WARRIORS!

True stories of combat, skill, and courage

by Jim Eldridge

SCHOLASTIC INC.

New York   Toronto   London   Auckland   Sydney
Mexico City   New Delhi   Hong Kong   Buenos Aires

No part of this publication may be reproduced in whole or in part, or stored in a retrieval system, or transmitted in any form or by any means, electronic, mechanical, photocopying, recording, or otherwise, without written permission of the publisher. For information regarding permission, write to The Chicken House, 2 Palmer Street, Frome, Somerset BA11 1DS, United Kingdom.

ISBN 0-439-29650-1

Copyright © 2001 by The Chicken House.
Text © 2001 by Jim Eldridge.
Illustrations © 2001 by Paul Fisher-Johnson.

All rights reserved. Published by Scholastic Inc., 555 Broadway, New York, NY 10012. The Chicken House is published in the United States in association with Scholastic.

SCHOLASTIC and associated logos are trademarks and/or registered trademarks of Scholastic Inc. THE CHICKEN HOUSE is a trademark of The Chicken House.

12 11 10 9 8 7 6 5 4 3 2 1   1 2 3 4 5 6/ 0

Printed in the U.S.A.
First Scholastic printing, September 2001

CONTENTS

1 50 A.D.: Roman Gladiators   6

2 1180 A.D.: Samurai   26

3 1485 A.D.: Knights in Armor:
   The Wars of the Roses   50

4 1836 A.D.: Texas: The Alamo   74

5 1991 A.D.: U.S. Special Forces:
   The Gulf War   90

6 2099 A.D.: Robot Wars   107

WARRIORS!

What is it that makes a good Warrior? Individual bravery? Loyalty? Skill?

Some become Warriors for the money – these are the mercenaries. Some become Warriors because they have no choice, they are forced into it – whether as a Gladiator in Roman times or a soldier in a drafted army.

Some become Warriors out of a sense of purpose and because they have a belief in what they are fighting for, a belief that is more important to them than life itself.

Whatever the reason, Warriors are at the front line, where that front line often means Death.

In such situations, to be a Warrior and survive calls for special skills. And to continue to be a Warrior and to go on surviving calls for someone who can live life on the very edge and know that every second may be the last.

These stories are based on some of the world's greatest Warriors. Are they admirable and brave, or are they mad and foolish? You decide!

1 ROMAN GLADIATORS

Roman gladiators were the outcasts of society: criminals, slaves, and prisoners of war. They fought to the death at public shows in Ancient Rome.

Often the gladiatorial contests would be part of a show that included chariot races and hunting and killing wild animals. The death rate at these events was enormous. The Emperor Trajan (who became Emperor in 98 A.D.) once staged a series of Games that went on for 120 days, during which over 5,000 men and 11,000 animals were killed.

The arenas the gladiators fought in were huge. The Circus Maximus, for example, could hold up to 250,000 people.

Gladiators who were mortally wounded were killed either by their opponents or sometimes by a man dressed as Charon, the mythical ferryman of the Underworld, who crushed their skulls with a heavy mallet.

Sometimes a gladiator could win his freedom if he showed bravery (and survived long enough!). Gladiators who were set free were given a wooden sword as a symbol of this honor.

THE HARDWARE

Velitis ("skirmisher") – a gladiator who wears no armor. His only weapon is a spear.

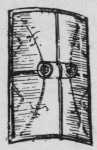

Retiatius ("net fighter") – a gladiator armed with a large net and a trident; sometimes his head is protected by a metal helmet.

Secutor ("pursuer") – a gladiator armed with a sword and wearing leg guards and armor on his sword arm. Also wears a helmet.

Samnium – gladiators from the Samnium region to the south of Rome. They were the most heavily armored of all gladiators.

GLADIATOR – 50 A.D.

The history behind the story

In 54 B.C., Julius Caesar's Roman army invaded southern Britain, although it wasn't until a hundred years later in 43 A.D. that the Romans – by now under the Emperor Claudius – carried out a full-scale invasion of Britain.

At this time, Britain was not one nation but a mixture of tribes, each ruled by their own separate King or Queen. There were more than 20 such tribes in what we know today as modern Britain.

As news of the latest invasion by the Roman forces spread north, the tribes prepared to defend themselves. Although the following story of Togod and Caradoc is invented, the tribe of the Silures (who lived in the area known today as south Wales) really did have a King called Caractacus who led his tribe against the Romans. The story of Togod is similar to other real stories that have been lost to us over 2000 years of history.

Togod the Briton stood on top of the bare hill. Surrounding him were hundreds more Britons, all armed with swords or spears.

The tall bearded figure of Caradoc, the first lieutenant of King Caractacus, rode backward and forward in front of them on his horse.

"Men of the Silures of Western Britain!" he shouted. "Today will be a great victory! Today we will face the Roman invaders and drive them from our lands! We will send them back to Rome!"

There were a few cheers from some of the men, but most of them, like Togod, were silent. They didn't want to be here. They wanted to be at home with their families or working their small patches of land, raising crops and tending their animals.

Togod remembered when the soldiers of King Caractacus had come to his hut.

"The Romans are marching toward us from the south," they had told him. "Your King needs all men to join him and fight."

"But I have my family to look after," Togod had protested.

Togod had called his family out to show the soldiers he was not lying. His wife, Aithne. Their eldest son, Brython, four years old. Their daughter, Cat, two. And the baby, Dob, just one year old, cradled in Aithne's arms.

"You can look after your family after we have beaten the Romans," snapped one of the men.

"But if I die in battle, who will care for them?" asked Togod desperately.

The sound of a horse's hooves made them all turn. That was when Togod first saw Caradoc.

Caradoc looked down at Togod and his family from his horse and then looked at the soldiers.

"What is the problem here?" he demanded.

"This man says he won't fight the Romans, sir," said one of the soldiers.

"No!" protested Togod. "I never said that. I just said that my family needed me here." He gestured toward two-year-old Cat. "My daughter has been ill. I have to work so that we can care for her."

Caradoc strode over to where Cat clutched Aithne's skirt.

Suddenly, before anyone was aware of what was happening, Caradoc had drawn a knife and had plunged it into the neck of the small girl, who fell to the ground.

Immediately, Aithne began screaming. She passed baby Dob to young Brython and grabbed up the body of Cat, hopelessly trying to stop the flow of blood.

Togod gaped, horror-struck. Then he threw himself at Caradoc in blind anger but was grabbed by three of Caradoc's soldiers. The three soldiers held the struggling man while Caradoc walked to his horse and climbed back onto it.

"There," he said. "You daughter is ill no longer. Now

you will fight with us against the Romans, or I will kill the rest of your family."

And Caradoc rode away.

The soldiers looked at Togod and at the weeping Aithne holding the dead body of their daughter.

"I am sorry," said one, gently. "But that is Caradoc's way."

"I will kill him!" raged Togod.

"No," said another soldier. "He will kill you. And then he will kill your family, as he says. If you want them to stay alive, come with us."

They let Togod go but kept their hands on their weapons in case the grief-stricken Briton should attack them.

Instead Togod went to his wife and put his arms around her.

"I must go with them," he told her. "If I don't, they will kill you as they killed our poor Cat. But I will come back after this battle is over. And we will start our life again."

With that, he released her and walked back to the waiting soldiers.

"I am ready," he said.

As he walked with them on their way to the next village to gather more conscripts for Caractacus's army, he thought of Aithne, and Brython, and Dob, and poor dead Cat. And he thought of the brutal face of Caradoc. And he vowed that if he ever got the chance, he would kill Caradoc.

Now, days later, Togod stood spear in hand and watched as his daughter's murderer, Caradoc, rode in front of him.

He wondered if he could manage to raise the spear

and hurl it at Caradoc before he was caught. But he knew that such an act would be useless. With the armor that Caradoc wore, only a spear thrust would be any good. And Caradoc was well guarded.

No, he would wait until after the battle. When things had quieted down. When the Romans had been beaten and gone home. Then Togod would find Caradoc and kill him.

Suddenly a shout was heard from the lookouts on another hilltop.

"The Romans!! The Romans are coming!!"

And there they were, marching in the valley about two miles away, the sun glinting on their armor.

"To your positions!" roared Caradoc.

Caradoc rode away, heading for where King Caractacus himself sat astride his horse.

Togod looked down into the valley at the advancing Romans. The column of shining metal, decked with flags and banners, seemed to be endless. There must be thousands of them, he thought. They will kill us all!

He clenched his spear firmly in his hand. Even in the cold air on the moors he could feel himself sweating with the fear of the battle that was to come.

But I will live through this, he told himself determinedly, because I have to kill Caradoc!

T he Roman sun beat down harsh and bright, but Togod didn't mind. Rather, he was grateful. Every day that he felt the hot sun on his skin meant he had survived another day. Another contest had been fought, and he had walked from the arena, alive.

It had been a year since the day of that battle on the misty moors of western Britain. The battle had been long and bloody. The Romans had formed their lines, and the British forces had attacked, shouting and screaming and hurling rocks to try and damage the Romans. But the Romans had protected themselves with their long shields.

Then the British, urged on by Caradoc, had run at the Romans, waving their swords and their spears. The Romans had simply stood and waited and, at a signal, had fired their arrows in force at the attacking warriors. Wave after wave of Britons had fallen.

And then, finally, the Romans had attacked, and the Britons had been cut down. Some, like Togod, had been taken prisoner and sent to Rome as slaves.

Togod never found out what had happened to his wife and children. There were rumors that after the battle, the Romans had put all the nearby villages to the sword, killing everyone and burning the villages to the ground. Togod never found out if it was true.

At first Togod found himself at sea as a galley slave, chained to the oar of a huge boat, rowing it across the sea to Rome. The whole time he rowed to the beat of the drum and had his back torn by the whip of the galley master, he was kept alive only by thoughts of one day getting back to Britain and finding out what had happened to Aithne, Brython, and Dob. There was also still

14

a feeling of deep hatred for Caradoc. He wondered if Caradoc had died, or if he had managed to escape. Chiefs nearly always escaped, he thought bitterly. It is only we common soldiers who die.

When Togod reached Rome he was sold as a slave to a builder. He spent long and painful hours digging rocks to be used in the huge buildings that were being put up all over Rome.

After a month of this, Togod's new master died suddenly. Poisoned, so rumor said, by a rival builder.

All the slaves, including Togod, were put up for sale. Among the bidders on the day of the sale was a large man with a broken nose and a scarred face. His name was Gallus.

"I'll have these six," Gallus had said, indicating Togod and five others as if he were buying cattle.

And cattle is what we are, thought Togod. Then he corrected himself. No, we are less than cattle. Cattle are valuable. We are just slaves. To work and die.

Togod and the other five men that Gallus had bought were tied together with a stout rope and then paraded through the streets as they followed Gallus on his horse. They walked for miles. Togod felt the hot sand and stones beneath his feet, but without pain. This past year as a Roman slave had made Togod's feet like tough leather.

Finally they reached their destination: a gladiator school at the edge of town.

"You men are the lucky ones!" Gallus told them. "You will be slaves no more. From now, you will be gladiators. I will train you. You will have the best of everything. Some of you will die in the arena. You should be grateful for that. Better to die as a gladiator than live as a slave. The strongest of you will live. Some of you may even gain your freedom, as I gained mine."

And so began a new phase in Togod's life, as a gladiator.

The year Togod had spent as a slave had given him new muscles and a hardened skin. He was able to take the blows and punishment that came with the training. As a slave he had already been taking such torment the past year. And none of the blows that landed on his body could equal the pain he'd felt when he'd seen young Cat die before his eyes at Caradoc's hands.

Togod's training as a gladiator sharpened his reflexes. First with the training machines: wooden contraptions that swung and whirled, swinging heavy wooden weights that the trainees had to dodge. After a few painful knocks, Togod learned to dodge them.

Then against the other trainees. Togod noticed that many of the other trainee gladiators rushed at their opponents. Togod learned to stay back from his opponent. Let his opponent make the first move, then dodge away and counterattack.

Then, finally, came the actual contests in the arena. Togod had fought in three so far, and at the end of each one he had left the arena with the other victorious gladiators, leaving their opponents dead on the sand behind them.

Togod hated the arena. Every time he entered it he felt the fear rise up within him as the question hung over him: Would this be the day he died?

So far he had been lucky. On his first time in the

arena he had drawn the retiarius, the trident, and the net, and had been pitted against a gladiator armed with a shield and sword. The other gladiator had become tangled up in Togod's net almost as soon as the contest had begun, and Togod didn't give the other man a chance to struggle free. He had plunged the forked prongs of the trident through the net into him.

On Togod's second contest he had been the one armed with the sword and shield and pitted against a retiarius. Having learned from experience, Togod took care to keep out of reach of the net as the other gladiator tried to catch him with it. In this way, by keeping on the move the whole time, he tired his opponent and wore him down. When Togod sensed that his opponent was struggling for breath, Togod hurled his shield at the other gladiator's legs, striking him painfully across the shin and bringing him crashing to the ground. Before the man could get up, Togod was on him with his sword.

His last contest had been close. This time he had been armed with just a spiked ball on a length of chain. His opponent had been armed with a spear.

Togod sensed that his opponent was wary about throwing the spear at Togod because if he missed he would be defenseless.

After much fighting, the other gladiator made a lunge at Togod. Togod swung his spiked ball and caught the spear in the chain, pulling it from his opponent's grasp and unbalancing him. As the man tumbled to the floor, Togod acted swiftly. There was no time for mercy in the gladiatorial arena. The quickest and the most ruthless survived.

Now, Togod practiced with the other gladiators in the hot Roman sun. This afternoon he was using a long wooden sword against a dummy. The dummy hung from a swinging wooden frame. Every swing of the dummy caused another wooden arm to swing out with two large wooden balls on ropes, capable of knocking a man unconscious if they struck him on the head. The skill was to strike the dummy and at the same time avoid being hit by the flying wooden balls.

It had been two weeks since Togod's last contest. Tomorrow he would enter the arena for his fourth.

Let me have the strength to win tomorrow and survive another day, Togod prayed silently as he thrust at the cloth dummy with the wooden sword. Let me win and be able to one day walk free from the arena and return home to my Aithne, my Brython, and my baby Dob.

Togod knew that to hope for such a thing was stupid, but here in Rome it was the only thing that kept him going: the desire to one day return to Britain and see his family once more. By then they would be old. He doubted if they would even recognize him. But it was this one wish that kept him going. That, and to find out what had happened to Caradoc.

Togod returned to attacking the swinging dummy with his wooden sword, watching out for the flying wooden balls that could hit him on the side of the head if he wasn't careful.

As he lunged successfully and then leaped back, he crashed into the figure of Gallus, who had just arrived behind him.

Gallus moved back from Togod, still light in his movements for a man of his age.

"My apologies, master," bowed Togod, always remembering who had power of life and death over him. "I did not see you there."

"Always keep your eyes everywhere, Briton," grunted Gallus. "That way you will stay alive in the arena."

"I have kept alive so far, and I hope to continue to do so," said Togod.

"Three contests and three victories," agreed Gallus. "But they were against feeble opponents." Gallus smiled. "Your next fight will be worthy of a gladiator. When you go into the arena tomorrow it will be against Aristos."

At the mention of this name, a whisper of awe could be heard among the other gladiators.

Aristos was the name of a gladiator from a town to the north of Rome. He had arrived in Rome some weeks before, following a spectacular series of victories in his own town. So far none of the gladiators had actually set eyes on this Aristos, although word about him had come to them from gossip and rumors and eyewitnesses who'd watched Aristos in training.

Some rumors said Aristos was a former Roman soldier who'd chosen the life of a gladiator. Other rumors had him to be the son of a wealthy Roman senator who'd been kicked out by his family in disgrace. Others said Aristos was a barbarian who'd been taken prisoner in a battle and fought as a gladiator in exchange for his life. Whatever the truth was, there was no doubt about Aristos's reputation as a fearless fighter. Stories from his hometown to the north of Rome said that Aristos had fought thirty times in the arena, sometimes against other gladiators, sometimes against wild animals. Each time he had been victorious.

Now his master had brought Aristos to Rome to fight. Already people were paying the highest prices for seats at the next Games, eager to catch sight of this famed and fearless Aristos in action. And Togod was to be his opponent.

The next afternoon, Togod sat on a wooden bench in one of the bare rooms beneath the huge Roman arena. He carried the net and trident and wore the metal helmet of the retiarius. That was the lot he had drawn. He wondered what the gladiator Aristos would be using. Sword? Spear? Axe? The spiked ball?

The Games had been going on for hours already. Through the grilles of the room he could hear the roars of the crowd, the screams of the dying.

The preliminary bouts had taken place. The chariot races. The contests between the wild animals and lightly armed gladiators. At each one the crowd had roared and yelled for more, but already Togod had started to pick up the beginnings of an expectant chant: "Aristos! Aristos!"

The crowd was eager to see the new favorite, the new champion.

Togod looked at the other gladiator in the room with him. Chan, a large man holding a spear, sat silently, thinking his own thoughts. Togod expected Chan was wondering who his own opponent would be. In another small cell further along the arena, Togod knew their two opponents would be sitting, thinking the same thing. This was to be a special contest for the audience, just four men in the arena: Chan against his opponent, and Togod against Aristos.

There was the sudden clarion call of trumpets sounding from out in the arena, then the heavy wooden door that separated Togod's cell from the arena was dragged open, and the harsh bright sunlight poured in.

A Roman soldier appeared in the doorway and gestured to Togod and Chan.

Togod put on his metal helmet, picked up his net and trident, and walked out, Chan following.

As Togod and Chan entered the arena a great roar went up from the crowd. Thousands and thousands of voices shouting and yelling and screaming, and the chant grew louder: "Aristos! Aristos! ARISTOS!!"

Then another door opened, and two men stepped out onto the hot sand. One was small but wiry. In his hand he held an axe. This was to be Chan's opponent.

The other had a sword and shield. He was tall and his head was shaved bare. Aristos.

Aristos turned, sword raised, to acknowledge the crowd. Togod caught the gladiator's profile, saw his eyes, and felt pain and anger combined with an overwhelming feeling of satisfaction surge through him. Aristos was Caradoc.

Although Caradoc had cut off his beard and mustache and had shaved his head in the Roman style, Togod knew he would never forget the eyes in that cruel face or the way that Caradoc walked.

Togod felt his grip tighten on the trident. He felt this desire to run at Caradoc with the trident and run him through. But no, he would wait. He wanted Caradoc to know who he was and why he was going to die.

The crowd's chant of "Aristos! Aristos!" continued, now added to by the stamping of thousands of feet and the clapping of thousands of pairs of hands in unison.

All eyes turned to the Emperor, Claudius, standing beneath the purple canopy near them. Claudius raised his right hand, and the chanting of the crowd died down a little. The four gladiators, Togod, Chan, the small man, and Aristos, turned toward where Claudius stood and each held up an arm in salute.

Claudius dropped his arm in a signal for the contests to begin. The Emperor sat down on his gilded throne, and the yells of the crowd and the chanting started up again.

Togod moved away from Chan and his opponent into a clear space. He wanted no obstacles when he threw the net.

Aristos gave a gesture of triumph toward the crowd with his sword and then faced Togod.

Togod had been in Aristos's position himself, armed with a sword and shield against a man with a net and trident. There were advantages and disadvantages to both.

The net and the trident were cumbersome. The sword was easier to handle, and the shield gave protection. However, the trident was long and could keep a sword-wielder at bay if used properly. And the net could tangle any opponent, provided it fell correctly. Against a seasoned fighter like Aristos, Togod knew he had one good chance. His throw had to be a good one, dropping his net over Aristos and catching him. If Togod missed, Aristos would grab the net, pull Togod off balance, and then strike. Togod knew that Aristos was fast with a blade, he'd seen that painfully and at close range a long, long year ago back in Britain.

Aristos lunged at Togod with his sword and then pulled abruptly back, hoping to catch Togod off balance. Togod saw the move coming, waited his time, and kept moving, circling around Aristos.

Togod found himself looking into Aristos's face and saw that the other gladiator was grinning. Togod realized with a shock that Aristos was actually enjoying himself. Aristos liked being in the arena!

The two men continued to circle each other. Out of the corner of his eye, Togod glimpsed Chan engaged in a bloody struggle with the small, wiry man, their weapons clashing against each other. He dismissed them from his consciousness and turned his attention fully to his opponent just in time. Aristos suddenly lunged again, whirling his sword in an arc at Togod. Togod barely had time to step back. He felt a sudden pain in the upper part of his left arm. He looked down. A gash had opened up and blood was pouring down his arm, soaking into the net that he held in his hand.

At the sight of this blood, the crowd went mad and their chant of "Aristos! Aristos!" increased in volume.

Aristos grinned broadly and came at Togod again; this time the blade of his sword sliced across Togod's back as he went past with a flourish.

Togod winced and bit his lip to stop crying out against the pain. It was true what Gallus had said. His last three opponents in the arena had been poor specimens. This man was something altogether different. A real fighter. A champion. Harder. Stronger. Tougher. Quicker. More ruthless. But Togod had one thing on his side that Aristos did not have – a thirst for revenge.

As Aristos came in for the third lunge to disable Togod further, Togod suddenly cried out "Caradoc!"

Any doubts that Togod might have had about Aristos' identity vanished at that instant, as Aristos stopped. His face betrayed him, the bewilderment at hearing this name. And Togod could tell that the man recognized the name. In the second that Aristos hesitated, Togod struck. The net flew out and dropped over Aristos. Togod immediately gave a sharp pull, and Aristos, vainly tying to cut his way out of the net, stumbled and fell to the sandy ground of the arena.

The crowd fell silent, shocked.

Togod advanced on Caradoc, the trident held high in his free hand.

"Who are you?" demanded the fallen gladiator, trying to claw his way out of the net.

By way of answer, Togod tore off his helmet and hurled it aside.

"I am Togod!" he announced. "And you are Caradoc, the murderer of my child and my family! And I have waited a very long time to see you again!"

With that Togod released the net and took the shaft of the trident in both hands.

"Prepare to die," he said. "And may the devils take you."

With that he plunged the trident down as hard as he could. Then he stood up, leaving the trident sticking up for all to see.

Now a new murmur came from the crowd, building in volume as the word went around the stadium from voice to voice, rising. Now Togod could hear them as they shouted: "Togod! Togod! Togod!"

As the chanting grew louder, Togod looked at the body of Caradoc, still caught up in the net.

Caradoc was dead. Tomorrow there would be more contests. More opponents. And he would win them all. Because he had to gain his freedom. He had to return home.

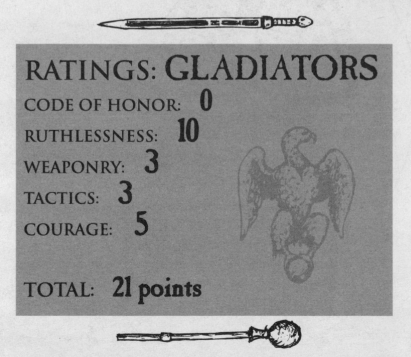

RATINGS: GLADIATORS

CODE OF HONOR: **0**

RUTHLESSNESS: **10**

WEAPONRY: **3**

TACTICS: **3**

COURAGE: **5**

TOTAL: **21 points**

2 SAMURAI

From earliest times, Japan was divided into areas ruled by different clans who were frequently at war with one another. Even within these separate areas, or provinces, different clans fought to gain power. To lead their armies, and also for their own protection, the Lords of these clans employed samurai warriors. Although samurai could be thought of as mercenaries, their code of honor distinguished them from soldiers who simply fought for money. To a samurai, his personal honor and code of conduct were all-important.

Samurai warriors were skilled in all kinds of fighting. In battle they wore highly decorative armor, adorned with the symbols of their masters.

THE HARDWARE

Samurai Swords

A samurai warrior had two swords: one long sword and one short.

The **katana** was the long sword, made to be used with two hands.

The **wakizashi** was the short sword, used in close combat, for thrusting like a dagger rather than as a cutting weapon (which was the case with the longer katana).

In both swords, a **tsuba** (sword guard) protected the hands, while cord twisted around the handle gave a secure grip.

Samurai warriors did not use a shield. They believed that their swords used properly were shield enough against an opponent.

Samurai Armor

Samurai armor was made from small scales made of iron or leather and tied together with silk or leather cords. The reason for this mix was because a suit made completely of iron would be too heavy to wear. The iron scales mainly covered the parts of the body that needed protection most.

The **do** (body armor) was made up of the back plate and the breast plate. There were many kinds of do.

The **kusazuri** was a laminated, protective skirt.

The **manju no wa** consisted of shoulder pads, collar, and armpit guards (**wakibiki**) all together in one piece.

In addition the samurai was protected by:

Nodawa
(throat protector)

Hoate
(mask)

Kabuto
(helmet)

Suneate
(shin guards)

Haidate
(thigh guards)

Yugake
(gloves)

Going to War

A samurai army going to war was a time for much ceremony. Before the army set off, Shinto prayers were offered to the Gods of War. Omens of good luck were looked for. For example, if the leader's horse turned in the direction of the enemy, this was considered a sign of good luck. If the horse turned toward the leader's own troops, this could be interpreted as bad luck, and many prayers would have to be said to try to counteract it.

The armies of the greatest war lords were often enormous, divided into separate companies, with sections for messengers, flag-bearers, musicians, archers, spear soldiers, bowmen, cavalry, and foot soldiers.

In 1589, the army of Toyotomi Hideoyoshi numbered over 200,000 men.

The army swept along in full ceremonial regalia, with gongs, bells, flags, and banners – a sight to strike fear into any opponent.

Samurai – 1180 A.D.

The history behind the story

In 1180, the Gempei Civil War occurred in Japan and involved many different clans. At the heart of the Civil War was a battle for the throne between the Taira clan of the young Samurai, Kiyomori, and the Minamoto clan, who supported Prince Mochito, a pretender to the throne. As with all civil wars, the country was split apart.

With so many battles and wars being waged, many pirates and organized bands of armed robbers took the opportunity of the Civil War to rob and plunder for their own gain. Although this story is fiction, it is based on events that happened during the Gempei Civil War.

The rain battered down on the roof of the small inn. Inside, the men were drinking their rice wine and talking of the weather and of bandits, when the door creaked open and a tall man entered. He was wet through from the rain, from his shaven head with its pigtail of hair tied at the back, down to his sandaled feet. But it was the two swords in his belt that held the attention of the drinkers in the inn. The long katana and the shorter wakizashi. Samurai swords. What was a strange samurai doing in this part of Masuda province?

The samurai approached the counter and inclined his head in a small bow of courtesy to the innkeeper.

"The rain is hard," he said quietly. His voice was low, but the stillness in the inn meant that everyone heard his words. "Is there anywhere in this village that I could take shelter?"

Before the innkeeper could answer, a voice from the shadows of the inn sneered out: "A samurai begging for shelter?"

The samurai turned and looked into the shadows, making out the shapes of three men seated at a table.

"I do not beg," replied the samurai simply. "I ask."

One of the three men stood up from the table and stepped onto the main floor of the inn, where he could be seen in the flickering light from the fire that burned in

the open grate. He was a tall man. Broad-shouldered. The scars that criss-crossed his face showed that he had been in many battles. And he had survived. As he looked at the stranger he sneered and then spat into the fire.

"A samurai without a home," he said mockingly. "A ronin."

The samurai inclined his head in acknowledgement. A ronin was a samurai without a master. There were many reasons why a samurai became a ronin, or a wandering samurai. Either his master's clan had been destroyed in battle, or his master had been disgraced, or the samurai had simply been dismissed.

The man with the scarred face gave a mocking laugh.

"A samurai without a master is either a fool or a criminal," he said. "Which are you?"

The samurai looked at the scarred man. If he was annoyed by the insults, his face didn't show it. Instead, he said calmly, "I do not need to give the reasons to you." Then he turned again to the innkeeper and asked: "My question was of shelter in this village . . ."

Before the innkeeper could reply, there was a roar of anger from the scarred man.

"Do not turn your back on me, ronin!" he shouted angrily.

He threw his leather cup at the samurai. The cup just missed the stranger, crashed into the counter, and fell to the floor.

A gasp was heard throughout the inn, and the samurai turned to see that the scar-faced man himself now held a long katana in both hands.

"I am Shigeoki! Samurai warrior of my master, Lord

Ashikaga! I won't have wandering criminals or fools in my province!"

The samurai stranger looked at the now-armed Shigeoki with a calm expression.

"I hope your aim with a sword is better than that with a cup," he said.

The ronin's calmness only made the scarred samurai even angrier.

"You shall find out as soon as you draw your own sword!"

The ronin looked at the angry samurai, then said quietly: "I have no quarrel with you. Your rudeness and lack of honor insult you, not me." Turning back to the innkeeper, he said, "I will find shelter elsewhere."

With that he stepped toward the door, but the angry Shigeoki was there ahead of him, using his long sword to bar the ronin's way.

"You are no samurai!" he spat. "You are a coward! A thief who has stolen a samurai's swords! Lay down your swords and perhaps I will let you go! Otherwise, use them and defend yourself!"

The wandering ronin stood still, his eyes on the angry samurai, but also aware of all the other eyes in the inn.

"You are drunk or stupid," said the ronin calmly. "Stand aside and you will live."

Shigeoki's face grew even redder with anger, making the scars on his face stand out like furrows.

"If you will not draw your sword, you will die where you stand!" he snarled.

With that, the blade of Shigeoki's long sword flashed in the firelight as he raised it, ready to bring it down on

the ronin. Afterward, no one in the inn could remember actually seeing the ronin pull his sword from its scabbard. All they saw was a movement too fast to follow, and then the ronin was standing, feet apart, his long sword held at arm's length in front of him.

Shigeoki swayed like a man drunk, and then, before the horrified gaze of the onlookers, Shigeoki's head fell to the floor, followed by his body crumpling on top of it.

In his palace, the Lord Ashikaga looked up from his battle plans as his Chief Minister, Yoshiko, entered the room, bowing all the while.

"Well?" demanded Ashikaga.

"We have him, master," nodded Yoshiko deferentially.

"Did he put up much of a struggle?" asked Lord Ashikaga.

Yoshiko looked uncomfortable. Before he could reply, a voice behind him said, "I came here of my own free will, my lord."

With that, the wandering ronin stepped forward into the room and bowed.

"I regret killing your samurai, but he left me with no choice. I would have preferred to go quietly on my way to find shelter. He insisted we fight or he would kill me."

Lord Ashikaga shot a look at Yoshiko, who gave a discreet nod to show that what the ronin had said was the truth.

Ashikaga looked at the ronin, taking in the man who stood quietly before him.

"How is it that you are without a master?" he asked.

"My master died," replied the ronin. "His widow decided to marry another Lord, with samurai of his own, so my services were no longer needed."

Lord Ashikaga studied the ronin as if trying to find out if the man was telling the truth. These were lawless times. There were many criminals and murderers about. Could this man be one of them, trying to worm his way into a noble house?

But then, this man had killed the feared Shigeoki, and with just one blow.

Ashikaga tapped the map lying on the table in front of him.

"Do you understand this?" he asked.

The ronin studied the map briefly, then nodded.

"It is a battle plan to take a castle on a mountain ridge," he said. He gestured to some of the marks that had been made in ink on the map. "The plan is to launch a full assault on the castle from the foot of the ridge." The ronin hesitated thoughtfully, then he added, his voice quiet and filled with careful respect. "This battle plan will fail."

Ashikaga gave the ronin a sharp look.

"Fail?!" he snapped. "How can you, who know nothing of the battle that is to come, nothing of the lay of the land or of the castle that is to be attacked, dare to say that this plan will fail?!"

"Because I have seen this style of battle plan before," answered the ronin. "It is a siege plan. The armies inside the castle need only defend themselves on one side, against the attacking army who are below them. The army inside the castle has the advantage. What is needed is for the assaulting army at the base of the mountain to be a diversion. The real attack should come from here." The ronin tapped a point on the map on the other side of the castle ". . . and here," tapping another point near to the first.

"Both of those positions are inside enemy territory," said Ashikaga. "The base of the mountain ridge is in my land and we can reach it safely."

The ronin bowed.

"The battle plan set out on your map will cost many lives and will fail," he said politely. "What are needed are two battalions under good and brave commanders to enter the enemy territory and take up their positions where I have indicated, near this upper gate, but remain under cover. As I have said, at the same time, a diversionary army is also based at the foot of the mountain.

"Meanwhile, a small band of warriors must enter the castle without being noticed. Once inside, their task is to open the two sets of upper gates . . . here . . . and here.

"As soon as the gates are open, the battalions lying in cover enter the castle."

Lord Ashikaga stood thoughtfully, looking down at the map and the impression the ronin's finger had left on the paper where he had marked his plan. Ashikaga looked at Yoshiko, but his Minister kept his head bowed and his eyes down.

Ashikaga looked out of the window, as if weighing things, then back at the map, and finally at the ronin, who had remained silent.

"I need a samurai to replace Shigeoki," said Ashikaga.

"I will be honored to serve your lordship," bowed the ronin.

Ashikaga nodded.

"Good," he said. "What is your name?"

The ronin now stood up straight and looked Ashikaga in the eye.

"My name is Bokudo," he said. "And I pledge my life to my new master, Lord Ashikaga."

Bokudo and Lord Ashikaga sat astride their horses, side by side on the hilly peak, and looked down on Ashikaga's army gathered in the valley below. On the top of the mountain ridge across the valley was their objective, a castle jutting out from the stone of the cliff. Thick, high wooden walls rose from the cliff, with black flags flying from the castle turrets.

The army in the valley below was just five thousand men, spread out to make it seem larger. Tents had been set up, more than were needed for five thousand men. Cooking fires were burning, the smoke curling up and filling the valley. This was another ruse of Bokudo's — smoke and many tents to make the enemy think that the valley held the whole of Ashikaga's army.

Already two separate contingents from Ashikaga's army were making their way through the woods on foot, up the mountain paths, inside enemy territory, heading for their positions under cover as near as they could get to the two sets of castle gates.

Down in the valley, flags were going up. Drums could be heard. Ashikaga's army was continuing the public displays of ceremony that had begun when they had set off from the palace: loud triumphant music, the clashing of steel as weapons were brandished challengingly at the enemy.

From this distance, Bokudo could make out figures appearing on the turrets of the castle, looking down into the valley. He could see the glint of spear tips in the sunlight from the castle.

Beside the samurai, Ashikaga suddenly spoke:

"You have not asked me why we are attacking this castle, Bokudo," he said Ashikaga.

"You are my lord and master," replied Bokudo with a bow of his head. "Your command is all I need to know."

Ashikaga fell silent again, and then he said: "I wish to tell you, anyway."

"As your lordship wishes," murmured Bokudo.

"The land where the castle sits belongs to no one lord. It used to belong to Lord Sezawa, but lately pirates and robbers have taken it over. They have made incursions into my lands. They have robbed and killed my peasants. Shigeoki was supposed to deal with them, but he failed. Then, last week, yet another band of robbers entered my lands. They came while my daughter, Suji, was visiting the border areas where the robbers last struck. She was seeing what damage had been done and finding out what needed to be done to help them, apart from more protection. She had gone without asking my permission. If she had done so, I would have refused. The border lands are too dangerous, especially with these robbers."

Ashikaga fell silent for a moment, and his gaze was full on the wooden and stone of the castle at the top of the mountain ridge in front of them. Bokudo said nothing, just sat on his horse and waited for his master to continue speaking.

"My daughter was taken by a party of robbers. One of her party escaped and returned to my palace with the news. The robbers are holding my daughter in that castle. They wish me to surrender my lands to them, or they will kill her." Ashikaga's face darkened. "I believe they will kill her, anyway."

"I believe so, too, master," nodded Bokudo. "That is often the way with robbers and pirates."

The samurai looked down at the army, at the castle, and then said firmly but quietly, "I will get your daughter back for you, master. Or I will die in the attempt."

Ashikaga nodded.

"I knew you would say that. And I believe if there is any man here who can do it, that man is you. How will you do it?"

Bokudo was silent for a while, then he said: "I will

lead the small force of men who will gain access to the castle. While the others open the gates, I will find your daughter and rescue her."

"She may already be dead," said Ashikaga somberly.

"She may," admitted Bokudo. "There is only one way to find out."

As darkness fell that night, Bokudo and three other men kept close watch on the castle gates from the cover of the trees. Bokudo had chosen his companions for this mission himself. First, he asked for volunteers who were ready to die for their master. From these he whittled the number down to a mere handful who showed they had excellent fighting and climbing skills. It was the climbing that was going to be all-important at first.

He had pitted this handful against each other in unarmed combat, watching for speed and agility and fearlessness. He had chosen three: the small but very powerful Edo, with his tiny body but long arms and hands like claws; the taller but equally wiry Tagenoshi; and the powerfully built figure of Matsu. Bokudo had armed each of his three companions with a short sword, a small bow, and a quiver of arrows. With these few weapons and the men's own physical abilities, Bokudo was sure he had a small but powerful force that could take on the might of the robbers in the castle.

The four of them had made their way up through the thick jungle of trees, up from the valley floor, keeping off paths and roads and traveling by half-tracks that only sheep and monkeys could use. On their way up, Bokudo had paused to check that both army battalions had gained their positions at the top of the mountain, near to the castle, and were well hidden. Then he and his companions had moved on to their final position, the edge of the jungle overlooking the castle itself.

"See that wall there," said Bokudo, pointing to a wall made of thick tree trunks that soared fifty feet above the rocks at its base. "Your task, Edo, is to climb that wall, using daggers the way I showed you. Do you think you can do it?"

The small wiry man nodded, his face serious.

"To save my lady Suji I would climb all the way to heaven," he said firmly.

"Just as far as the top of the wall will do," said Bokudo. "Once there, fix the rope and let it down. We will join you."

Bokudo strained his ears to listen to the sounds coming from the castle. Most of the noise seemed to be coming from the far side, from the turrets that looked down onto Ashikaga's army in the valley below. Darkness was now complete. The moon was hidden behind clouds.

"Go," whispered Bokudo.

The small wiry man scuttled out from the cover of the trees, crouching low. Bokudo, Tagenoshi, and Matsu watched Edo as he moved away from them. Under cover of darkness they could barely see him as he reached the wooden walls of the castle.

Bokudo strained his eyes in the darkness. Yes, he could just make out the dim shape in the darkness that was Edo. The small man pushed the two daggers into the wood just above the height of his head, hauled himself up, and gripped the timbers of the wall with his bare feet. Then he took one of the daggers out from the wall and pushed it in further up, following it with the second dagger, at the same time pushing himself up from his feet. It was a hard task that could only be done by someone light and agile, with strong arms and feet.

Soon Edo had disappeared into the darkness at the top of the wall.

Under the cover of the trees, Bokudo, Tagenoshi, and Matsu listened, waiting to hear sounds of a struggle or a shout that would tell them that Edo had been caught. No shout came. Instead, there was a movement at the bottom of the wall, and then they saw the dim outline of the rope hanging down. Edo had made it.

Swiftly, Bokudo and his two companions ran to the rope and began to climb up, hand over hand, feet walking upward against the timber of the wall.

Soon they had joined Edo at the top, on the walkway that ran around the top of the wall.

"You three open the gates," whispered Bokudo. "I will find her ladyship Suji, and then I will join you at the gates."

The men were just about to move off when they heard heavy footsteps approaching along the walkway. Immediately they shrank back into the shadows, but there was little cover to hide them. A startled voice began to call out "What are you . . . ?!"

Then there was the twang of a bow as Bokudo let fly with an arrow, and a gurgling choking sound, then a thud as the guard fell to the floor.

The four men hurried over to the fallen robber. He was dead. Bokudo's arrow had taken him right through the heart.

"It is rare for there just to be one guard on his own," muttered Bokudo. "They mostly work in pairs."

No sooner had Bokudo spoken than another man appeared. This man staggered back, shocked, and automatically began to draw his sword. Bokudo stopped Matsu as the big man drew his own bow.

"We need this one alive," said Bokudo. Turning to the guard, he snapped, "Put away your sword!"

The guard took one look at the four armed men and pushed his sword back into its scabbard.

"Tell us where the lady Suji is being kept prisoner," said Bokudo.

The guard looked frightened.

"I cannot! They will kill me if I tell!"

"I will kill you if you do not," said Bokudo. He pointed to the body of the dead guard, laying on the walkway. "He would not tell me."

The terrified guard looked at the dead man, and then he nodded.

"I will take you to her," he said.

"Good," said Bokudo. "But if you try to trick me, or shout out, you will be dead before your tongue has had a chance to move. Understood?"

Too afraid to open his mouth, the guard nodded.

Bokudo gestured to his three companions.

"To your tasks," he said. "I will see you later."

Edo, Tagenoshi, and Matsu hurried off to find the way to the gates. Bokudo gestured to the guard to lead the way down into the main body of the castle.

As they climbed down wooden ladders to the lower parts of the castle, Bokudo saw that the place was becoming a ruin. Litter and filth were everywhere. Lord Ashikaga had told him that robbers had taken over the castle from Lord Sezawa. From the mess that lay around, Bokudo felt that these robbers were little more than ill-disciplined barbarians. An army man would be ashamed to let his base fall into such a state. These robbers were just a rabble, however good they might be as fighters.

Bokudo followed the robber guard along a torchlit passage. At the end was a door. Outside the door stood two men, each armed with a spear and with the hilt of a sword protruding from a scabbard.

They looked up and nodded as they recognized the guard, then frowned as they saw Bokudo behind him.

"He has come to rescue the woman!" yelled the guard, and with that he threw himself desperately away from Bokudo and toward his two robber-accomplices, pulling his sword from his scabbard as he did so.

The split second of shocked confusion between the two guards gave Bokudo the briefest of advantages, and he took it. Almost faster than the eye could see, he had whipped his long sword from its scabbard behind his back and chopped down with it, cutting down one of the guards before he could draw his sword.

The second guard jabbed fiercely at Bokudo with his spear. Bokudo swerved to one side and, as the spear scraped past him, sprang forward, at the same time sweeping his sword in an arc. The second guard collapsed to the floor.

Bokudo turned to the third man, cowering back against the door, his sword drawn.

"I said I would kill you if you tried to trick me," said Bokudo. "A samurai always keeps his word."

With that Bokudo's sword flashed in the torchlight. The third man barely had time to make a sound. Then he, too, lay dead on the floor.

Bokudo examined the door. It was locked. He slid his long sword back into its scabbard and stood for a moment studying the door. Then he raised his right foot and crashed it against the lock. The lock shattered and the wooden door caved inward.

Bokudo snatched one of the torches from its holder in the passage wall and entered the room. Inside the tiny cramped room, a young woman sat on the bare floor. Beneath the dirt that stained her, Bokudo could see that her clothes were of the finest material. This had to be Lord Ashikaga's daughter.

"My lady Suji," bowed Bokudo. "Your father, Lord Ashikaga, has sent me to retrieve you. My name is Bokudo."

"But how . . . ?" began the startled young woman.

"I am afraid there is no time now for explanations, my lady," said Bokudo quietly. "We must first make our way out. Follow me."

The two hurried out of the small room, but even as they did so, they stopped. A robber had obviously heard the sounds of the scuffle in the passageway and had come to investigate. Now he stood looking at the three dead men on the floor and at Bokudo and Suji.

"We are under attack!" yelled the robber, drawing his sword. But Bokudo was already onto him, drawing his own long sword and thrusting with it. The man collapsed, but Bokudo could hear the sounds of many more robbers approaching, brought by the man's cry of alarm. He could hear the clang of metal as spears were prepared, hear the swish of many swords being drawn from their scabbards.

"Get back into the room, my lady," commanded Bokudo. He took a stance in the narrow passage, his long sword at the ready in one hand, his short sword in the other.

Suddenly the narrow passage was filled with robbers, all heavily armed. Bokudo pointed both of his swords toward them.

"In this space you are all at a disadvantage," he said coolly. "If you do not wish to die, surrender."

"Surrender to one man?!" jeered one of the robbers mockingly, and he leaped forward with his spear. With one forward stroke of his long sword Bokudo cut through the spear, and with his backward stroke cut through the man, who crumpled to the ground.

The other robbers looked at each other, worried. This samurai was a master with his swords. That was testified to by the fact that there were already four dead men here in this passage.

"He's just one man!" roared one angry robber. "If we rush him all at once he can't kill us all!"

"Would you care to put that to the test?" asked Bokudo, readying himself for their attack.

The robbers hesitated, and then from out in the body of the castle courtyard they heard the sound of trumpets and the beating of drums. Behind the sounds of the loud music they could also hear shouts and yells and the sounds of battle. Edo, Tagenoshi, and Matsu must have managed to open the gates, and now Ashikaga's two battalions were pouring in.

"Lord Ashikaga's army is inside your castle!" Bokudo announced triumphantly.

His words struck panic into the robbers in the passage. As one, they turned and fled along the passage, heading for the courtyard, some eager to join the battle, others desperate to escape from the castle out into the surrounding countryside.

Bokudo sheathed his short sword, but kept his long sword ready against further attacks.

"You can come out now, my lady!" he called.

Suji appeared from the tiny room.

"I heard what you said. Is it true? Is my father here?" Bokudo nodded.

"His army has entered the castle. He will not be far behind. If you follow me, I will take you to him."

The battle inside the castle was brief. Caught by the surprise attack, the robbers were soon overrun and defeated by Ashikaga's soldiers.

Afterward, with Lord Ashikaga joyously reunited with his daughter, Bokudo stood with Edo, Tagenoshi, and Matsu and watched as Ashikaga's army began rounding up the remaining robbers as prisoners, to be taken by Ashikaga as slave workers. Others began to collect the gold and jewels the robbers had stolen.

"It is your victory," murmured Matsu to Bokudo. "Do you never wish for the gold and wealth that come from taking an enemy's lands and castles?"

Bokudo shook his head.

"Gold and jewels are of no real value," he said quietly. "For a samurai, true worth lies in the honor of being a warrior."

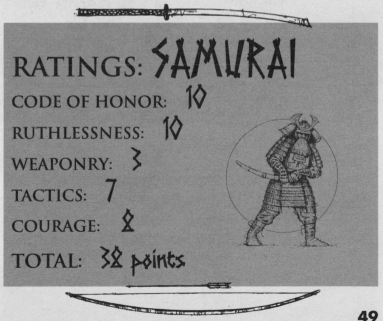

RATINGS: SAMURAI

CODE OF HONOR: 10

RUTHLESSNESS: 10

WEAPONRY: 3

TACTICS: 7

COURAGE: 8

TOTAL: 38 points

3 Knights in Armor

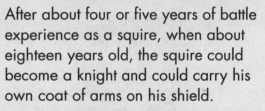

Knights were traditionally young men from titled families. The path to being a knight was in three stages:

First, a boy from an aristocratic family with a talent for fighting became a page at about the age of seven. As a page, he learned how to ride a horse properly and how to use various weapons – although at this stage the weapons were made of wood or their sharp edges were blunted.

Next, the page became a squire to a knight. This usually happened at about fourteen years of age. It was the squire's job to help his knight get ready for battle and to fight alongside his knight.

After about four or five years of battle experience as a squire, when about eighteen years old, the squire could become a knight and could carry his own coat of arms on his shield.

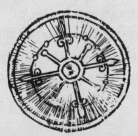

The Hardware

Armor

At first, in medieval times, knights wore chain mail covering their whole body, for their protection when they rode into battle. Chain mail was made up of rings of metal fixed together, but it could be pierced by arrows or the thrust of a spear. Because of this danger, plates of steel began to be used for greater protection.

By the 15th century a knight's suit of armor consisted of:

Helmet – including a visor, which could be raised

Bevor – protecting the chin and throat

Breastplate – protecting the upper front body, the stomach, and the tops of the thighs

Pauldron – protecting the shoulders

Besagew – a small metal sheet covering the gap in the joint between the body armor and that of the arm. In this way the armpit was protected against a thrust when the sword arm was raised in attack.

Vambrace – again, a joint protector, this time covering the chink in the elbow

Gauntlet – a metal glove protecting the hand and wrist

Cuisse – protecting the thigh

Greave – protecting the lower leg

Sabaton – metal shoes

Arming doublet – a jerkin made of cloth or leather, worn beneath the breastplate as added protection

Chainmail – worn beneath the armor on the whole upper body as further protection

The whole suit of metal weighed about 65 pounds, which made it difficult for a knight to move quickly on foot.

The knight's shield was usually made of strong wood, with leather straps at the back. The shield was to protect the knight against arrows and direct thrusts with lances or swords.

Weapons

Swords

Swords varied, depending upon what they were to be used for and the particular preference of the individual knight. The longest was the **great sword**, which was about four feet long. This was so heavy it needed two hands to use it successfully. Smaller than this was the standard two-edged **sword**, and then there was also the **falchion**, which was a single-edged broad-bladed sword only used for a chopping action.

Other Weapons

These other weapons included a **dagger**, or sometimes a short sword, for stabbing; a **mace**, a metal-headed club on a wooden handle; a **flail**, which was a spiked ball on a chain fixed to a wooden handle; an **axe**; and a **lance.**

There were two sorts of bows in use:

The **longbow**, which took strength to pull. A good archer could fire up to seven arrows a minute using a longbow.

The **crossbow** used bolts, or quarrels (short darts), and had a range of about 820 feet. Because it had a mechanism that had to be rewound after every bolt was fired, a crossbow archer could only fire about one bolt a minute.

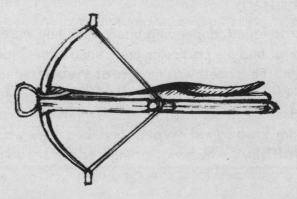

Knights in Armor: 1485 A.D.: The Wars of the Roses

The history behind the story

The Plantaganets had ruled England since 1154. At the end of the fourteenth century, the Plantaganet Richard II was deposed and later murdered by Henry IV, who became the first of the Lancaster kings. After Henry IV came his son, Henry V, and when he died, his one-year old son, Henry VI, officially became king.

However, as he grew older, Henry VI proved to be a weak king, and in his 30s he began to suffer bouts of insanity. During his reign, law and order in England broke down; Henry VI lavished fortunes on his favorites, and to pay for this royal spending, taxes were increased, which led to uprisings. These were brutally suppressed.

Soon the rival branches of the royal family, the Yorks and the Lancasters, were battling over who would gain control of the King and of the royal purse.

The Lancastrians were led by Henry VI's French wife,

Margaret of Anjou, a much more powerful figure than her weak husband, and by the Duke of Somerset.

The Yorkists were led by Richard, Duke of York (who until 1455 had been Lord Protector of England and heir to the throne), backed by the powerful Neville family, led by the Earl of Warwick.

In 1455, the feud between the Lancasters and the Yorkists broke into open warfare with the Battle of St. Albans, which the Yorkists won. However, Henry VI held on to the throne.

For the next three decades, England was in a state of Civil War as first one side, then the other gained ascendancy. This became known as the Wars of the Roses.

Richard, Duke of York, died in 1460. In 1461, following a Yorkist victory at the Battle of Towtown, Richard's son, Edward, deposed Henry VI and declared himself King Edward IV. In 1470, following Lancastrian victories, Henry VI was restored to the throne but was murdered in 1471. Once again, Edward IV became king, until his death in 1483. His brother Richard III then took over the throne.

By 1485, there was a new head of the House of Lancaster, Henry Tudor. He had spent most of his life in exile in Wales and Brittany, along with many other members of the Lancaster family. Now he was determined to come to England with his troops and try to take the crown of England away from the Yorkists. We may not know the exact details of what happened, but the great battle and characters in this story are all true.

"Curse Henry Tudor! May he die a beggar's death and the rats feast on his body!"

King Richard III of England paced around the royal chamber, his hand crumpling the sheet of paper that had brought him the bad news. Henry Tudor had landed in Wales some days ago and was already making his way through north Wales, heading for the border with England.

"This upstart has been in Wales for days already! Days! Why did no one tell me of his coming before? I was told he was still hiding in France! Do we not have spies? What do we pay them for?"

John Howard, Duke of Norfolk, watched his King as he raged. Then he replied calmly: "Unfortunately, Henry has many supporters in Wales. However, I believe his army is small. He has brought 3,000 men with him from France. An army of that size can be crushed easily."

"But what of the men who will join him on his way?" demanded Richard. "His army could be ten thousand strong by the time he reaches London!"

Norfolk shook his head.

"Many of the Lords are wary of joining Henry at this stage," he said. "Our spies tell us that most of them plan to wait and see what will happen between you and Henry before they decide who they will support."

"Don't talk to me about your spies!" stormed Richard. "They didn't even know that Henry had landed in Wales!" He paced, thinking over what Norfolk had said. He knew it had a grain of truth in it. He knew he was unpopular among many of the Lords. But he also knew that they were afraid of him. The many executions he had carried out for treason since he had taken the throne had made them all watch their words.

"They'll stand aside and support the one who wins!" spat Richard at last. "They are cowards all!"

He made a decision.

"We will raise our army and go and meet this upstart, this pretender to the throne, on the field of battle before he has a chance to increase the size of his army. I will cut his head off and put it on a spike outside the palace. Then everyone will know what happens to those who try to take the throne of England!"

Henry Tudor, Duke of Richmond, sat outside his tent and thought about the battle that was to come. Elsewhere in the camp his army was going about its business: eating, drinking, and preparing weapons, while he made his plans.

Now that his campaign was actually under way, Henry couldn't help but feel a sense of fear. This would be his first real battle. So far his fighting experience as a knight had been in minor campaigns, small skirmishes. The battle to come would test him to the limit. Not just his courage and his fighting skills, but his ability to lead.

He had 3,500 men. Three thousand had landed with him from France, the other 500 had joined him on his march north through Wales, and then east toward Shropshire. Henry was disappointed, he had hoped for more. He needed more. Richard had an army of 10,000 at his disposal, with more if some of the Lords joined him.

The Lords were the key to this campaign. If they supported him, then Henry would win. If they gave their support to Richard, then Richard would win. So far, most of them were doing nothing, just waiting.

Had he made a mistake in launching this attack, Henry wondered? He had been promised support by Rhys ap Thomas, the Welsh Lord, but so far there had been no sign of any men.

"Is there any word yet from Lord Stanley, Henry?" asked a voice.

Henry turned. His army chief-in-command, Lord Oxford, had appeared. It was a relief to Henry to have a seasoned battle campaigner and warrior like Oxford at his side.

Henry shook his head.

"No," he said. "I expect he waits to see what happens. He always was a careful man."

"A careful and powerful one," added Oxford.

Lord Thomas Stanley was Henry's stepfather. Henry had written to his mother begging her to get her husband to support him in his quest. But, as Oxford said, Lord Stanley was a careful man. He had survived the Wars of the Roses this long time by switching sides, each time choosing the more powerful, the new victor. He had built up his own army into one of the most powerful in England. There was no way of knowing which side Lord Stanley would support when it came to the battle.

"We are outnumbered, Oxford," said Henry with a heartfelt sigh. "I calculate that Richard has a two-to-one advantage over us, at the very least."

"Numbers are not always the most important factor," said Oxford. He gestured at the camp, at the rows of tents that had been put up around them. "The men we have are dedicated to our cause."

"The mercenaries are dedicated to the money," said Henry ruefully.

Oxford nodded in reluctant agreement. Henry's force was made up of 500 English exiles dedicated to the Lancastrian cause, 1,500 French soldiers, and 1,000 mercenaries, mostly Scots.

"But they are professional soldiers," Oxford pointed out. "They will fight well. And I believe more will join us."

"They had better," said Henry moodily. "There is more than just the crown at stake, there is the whole future of England."

Richard III, King of England, rode north. Beside him, astride their magnificent horses, were his lieutenants, John Howard, Duke of Norfolk, and Henry Percy, Earl of Northumberland. Behind them, also on horseback, came their squires and pages, and behind them, some on horse, some on foot, came the soldiers. An army 10,000 strong, marching north along the old Roman Road. Another 5,000 soldiers were on their way from the north to join them.

They were nearing Northampton now. Richard wondered how long it would be before they came upon Henry's army. According to his spies, Henry and his troops were camped at Shrewsbury, just barely into England from across the Welsh border. Some of the Welsh Lords had now joined Henry, but not enough to make Henry's army into a threat.

"Which way will Lord Stanley jump, John?" Richard asked his aide.

The Duke fell silent while he thought it over, then he said: "I think he will either join us or stay out of the battle."

"But Henry is his stepson," Richard pointed out. "And Henry's mother, Margaret Beaufort, is a strong-willed woman who rides roughshod over her menfolk."

"I doubt if she will ride roughshod over Thomas Stanley," said the Duke. "He is too careful of keeping his head on his shoulders. He is also very careful with his money. He would not risk being part of a campaign that could cost him dearly either way."

"The people will not support this Henry Tudor," put in Northumberland. "His claim to the throne is too thin. He is just another bastard from the illegitimate line of John, Edward III's son. That is no basis for kingship."

Richard fell silent, reflecting that at one time his own claim to the throne had also been "thin." Richard's brother Edward had become King, following the overthrow of that puny weakling, Henry VI. After Edward had died there had been other claimants to the throne. Edward's young son, for example. At 12 years old, he had been too young to take over the crown, so Richard had taken command of the throne as Lord Protector on the boy's behalf. Later the boy had been murdered, as had his younger brother, Prince Richard. There were rumors that Richard had ordered their murders.

There had also been Richard's brother, the Duke of Clarence, who had been killed on Richard's orders; and Clarence's children declared illegitimate to bar them from the throne.

Richard knew that these many deaths of people so close to him had helped make him feared and unpopular. But fear helped keep people in their place. When he defeated this pretender, this Henry Tudor, and destroyed his army, he would do it in a way that would make everyone fear him even more.

Rain, groaned Henry as his army trudged its way over muddy roads. Rain, which makes weapons slippery and difficult to hold. Which makes the ground wet and hard to keep a firm grip on when fighting.

"This rain will be the ruin of us," he grumbled to Oxford. Oxford shook his head.

"Rain is a leveller," he said. "It will make it as hard for Richard's troops."

"A curse on Richard," scowled Henry. "He has much to

pay for. He has killed many of our own families and enough of his own side to give him enough enemies to out-number him by thousands. Why are they not with us?!"

"They are afraid," said Oxford. "They know that those who oppose Richard die." Tentatively, Oxford asked, "Still no word from your stepfather?"

Henry shook his head.

"No word from him, nor his brother, William." He sighed. "If we only had their two armies with us, we would be so much stronger than Richard's army." Even with the addition of the army of the Welsh Lord, Rhys ap Thomas, their force only numbered just over 5,000. With reports coming in of Richard's army being 12,000, and even 15,000, strong, the odds against them were great indeed.

"Where is Richard's army now?" asked Henry.

"According to our scouts, he has made camp just east of Leicester, outside a village called Market Bosworth," replied Oxford. "We will be there by nightfall."

"So, tomorrow, we fight."

"Tomorrow we fight," nodded Oxford.

August 22, 1485. Bosworth Field. Dawn.

Richard III stood in his command tent, musing on the coming battle, as his squire and page dressed him in his armor. First the leather doublet, then the chainmail, and then, piece by piece, the steel plates to protect his legs, his body, his arms, his feet, his hands, his shoulders, leaving no chink for a stray arrow to penetrate.

Then his weapons: the sword heavy in its scabbard, hanging from his luxuriously decorated leather belt. A dagger in a smaller scabbard.

Finally his helmet was put in place.

Richard stood before the mirror held by his page and saw his own reflection. He knew he was every inch the knight, the warrior king.

"Open the velvet bag in my box," he ordered his squire.

The squire did so and revealed a crown adorned with jewels. A King's crown.

The squire placed it on Richard's head, fitting it over the crown of his master's helmet.

Richard looked at his reflection once more in the mirror. Yes, now he was the Warrior King.

The curtains of his tent parted and the Duke of Norfolk entered and bowed.

"The enemy are gathered, sire," he said.

"How large is Henry's army?" asked Richard.

"Our spies were right, about five thousand men. Our forces outnumber them three to one."

"So Lord Stanley is not with them," said Richard, pleased.

The uncomfortable look that came into Norfolk's face made Richard frown.

"Or do you have news about Lord Stanley?" he asked, suspiciously.

"Lord Stanley and his army are also on the field, as is the army of his brother, William Stanley. They have four thousand men with them."

"Treason!" raged Richard. "They dare to rise against their King!"

Norfolk shook his head.

"They say they will take no part in the battle on either side," said Norfolk.

"Then why are they here?" demanded Richard. "And in such force?"

"If their past record is anything to go by, it is to see who is winning, and then join in on the winning side and take their share of the spoils," said Norfolk.

Richard nodded.

"The Stanleys are nothing but parasites and criminals!" he scowled. Grudgingly, he added: "But we need them to stay out of the fight. If they come in on Henry's side it could put us at risk." He shook his head in disgust. "There is treachery everywhere, Norfolk. A King cannot trust anyone these days!"

A few miles away, Henry Tudor and Lord Oxford watched as their commanders assembled their troops on the western side of Bosworth Field.

From this distance they could see that Richard's army had already taken the higher ground of Ambion Hill.

At the front of Richard's troops was a contingent of archers, on foot. Behind them, on horseback, were at least 2,000 men in armor, their weapons gleaming in the early light of the morning sun's rays.

On either side of the hill, running from the ridge at the top to the marshy ground at the bottom, were lines of cannons, about 150 on each side. Chains could be seen fixing each cannon to the next cannon, making an explosive defensive fence to stop riders attacking from the sides of the hill.

Stretching up to the top of the hill, behind the archers and the mounted horsemen, were many thousands more men in armor, some on horseback, some on foot. All were armed with lances, pikestaffs, and swords.

And, to one side, the mounted armies of Lord Thomas Stanley and his brother, William Stanley, like spectators at a game.

"Your stepfather is here," commented Lord Oxford drily.

"But whether to support me or to oppose me depends on how we do," said Henry, and for the first time he gave a grin of amusement at his situation.

The shouts of command from Henry's side were continuing in English, French, Gaelic, and Welsh as the different troops were ordered into battle formation by their commanders.

"We will have to be the ones to attack," said Oxford.

"I know," nodded Henry in agreement.

"May I have the honor of leading the attack?" asked Oxford.

Henry looked for a moment as if he was going to argue, then he nodded.

"I would be honored for you to take that role," he said. "You are more experienced in battle. I would hate to make a grave mistake so early in the day and lose us the whole battle before it has barely begun. How will you proceed?"

Oxford studied the ranks of Richard's army from a distance and then pointed out the cannons.

"The cannons that Richard has placed for the protection

of his troops could also be their undoing. They narrow their front, cutting down the number of men who could attack us. At the same time the chains prevent their troops from breaking out and attacking us down the sides of the hill. Also, it is difficult to fire a cannon *down* a hill. I shall attack on all three sides of the hill at once."

"Richard's archers will account for many of our men."

"Then we will have to see what we can do with the rest," said Oxford.

By now the sun had risen higher in the sky. Morning was well under way. The battle lines were now complete and ready, waiting.

Henry held out his mailed hand and shook Oxford's gauntlet.

"Good luck," he said. "And may God give us victory on this day."

"To King Henry," said Oxford.

Then he wheeled his horse and rode toward the front of the assembled troops.

From their position on the top of the hill, Richard and Norfolk watched as Oxford split Henry Tudor's troops into three groups and spread them across the base of the hill. Two of the groups moved to the sides of the hill, directly beneath Richard's two lines of cannons. Oxford stayed at the head of the middle group, now directly beneath Richard's position.

"Surely Oxford cannot mean to launch an attack so soon?" queried Richard. "And where is Henry?"

"I see him with the troops at the rear," said Norfolk.

"Ha! Hiding!" spat Richard scornfully.

A sudden roar went up from the troops at Henry's front

line, and then they were rushing up the hill, Oxford at their head on his charger, waving his sword.

"We have begun!" growled Richard. With that he raised his own sword and yelled, "Forward! Fire the cannons!"

Richard was just about to urge his own horse down the slope toward the battle, but Norfolk stopped him.

"Not yet, sire," he appealed.

"You think I am afraid?!" demanded Richard angrily.

Norfolk shook his head.

"I know you are not, but an unlucky arrow at this early stage . . ."

Richard scowled.

"I am King! I lead my troops, I do not hide behind them, like Henry Tudor!"

With that Richard pulled down the visor of his helmet, and with a cry of "Richard!!" he dug his knees into his horse's side and urged it down the hill.

Norfolk groaned ruefully, and then followed his king, his own sword swinging heavily in his metaled fist.

As Oxford had predicted, the cannons at each side of the hill were having problems. Their shots fired into the air, over the heads of Henry's advancing soldiers. Damage was done to Henry's soldiers at the rear of the column, but already the vanguard were at the chains that held the cannons and were deep in hand-to-hand fighting, swords flying and chopping, pikes and lances thrusting.

Oxford and his troops, attacking the central part of the hill, were also making headway.

In the rear of his lines of soldiers waiting in reserve,

Henry gritted his teeth impatiently. This was no way for a King to behave, lurking in hiding! Whatever Oxford said, now was his time. Already he could see Richard swooping down on his great horse, the jewelled crown on his helmet clear for all to see.

Henry turned to his squire.

"Go to Lord Stanley," he said urgently. "Tell him our plan is succeeding and that I will now face Richard myself, and after my victory I hope to be able to call him my friend."

As his squire rode off toward the armies of the Stanleys, Henry smiled to himself at his choice of words. "I hope to be able to call him my friend." A politician like Lord Stanley would know only too well what Henry meant: If you do not bring in your soldiers on my side now, you are not my friend. And if you are not my friend, you are my enemy.

By now Henry could see that Richard was in the thick of the battle, his sword laying about him on all sides. Richard was fighting like a man possessed, a man with everything to lose.

"And I," thought Henry, as he pulled down the visor of his helmet and urged his horse forward, "am a man with everything to gain."

A loud cheer went up from Henry's troops as they saw their champion entering the battle, sword raised, his armor burnished in the sunlight that was now breaking through the clouds.

Richard heard the cheer and took a moment to look toward the sound and saw Henry racing on his horse toward him.

"Good!" he thought. "At last! This is the way it should be! Warrior against warrior!"

Richard wheeled his horse and headed toward the oncoming Henry, cutting a swath through the battle with his flashing sword, riding down those who stood in his way beneath the hooves of his horse.

The battle was now in full flood, the clash of weapon against armor, sword against shield. The air was filled with the screams of the wounded and dying.

Richard chopped down with his sword at a soldier who tried to rush at him with a spear, hacking the end off the spear with his downward blow, and then dispatching the soldier with his return blow, upward and outward.

Then, out of the corner of his eye, he saw what he had dreaded. Lord Stanley and his brother had brought their armies into the fray and were attacking Richard's men!

"Traitors!" he roared. "I will have you gutted!"

Suddenly he felt his horse stagger. As he looked, he saw a French soldier had thrust a pike deep into his horse. Richard swayed in the saddle, and then his horse crumpled beneath him, throwing Richard as it crashed to the earth.

"Richard is down!!" went up the cry.

"Richard lives!!" Richard shouted, and he staggered to his feet, hampered by the weight of his armor.

A glancing blow hit him in the back and he stumbled, then turned and hacked with his sword at the man who had hit him.

A shadow fell over him and he looked up to see Henry Tudor astride his horse, sword raised.

Moving as fast as his armor would allow him, Richard

snatched up a fallen pike and thrust it up toward Henry. Henry swayed in his saddle to avoid Richard's thrust and then brought down his sword, but missed, the blade clanging harmlessly off Richard's armor.

Another thrust by Richard with the long pikestaff hit Henry full in the chest, and Henry tumbled backward, crashing to the ground in a smashing of metal against metal.

Henry's horse whinnied and reared and then backed away.

Henry hauled himself to his feet, his sword still held in his hand.

Richard tossed the pikestaff aside and flexed his own sword.

"At least, Henry Tudor, you will die like a man," snarled Richard, and he lashed out at Henry.

Henry brought his own sword up and deflected Richard's blow with it, the clang of metal ringing out.

Again Richard attacked, the force of his blows forcing Henry back, as this time his blade smashed down on Henry's armor. But though his flailing sword crashed and banged and bruised Henry, it could not find a gap in the metal protection.

Henry retreated, giving further ground against Richard's blows, and then, as Richard gave one last swinging downward blow aimed at the top of Henry's helmet, Henry swayed to one side. The momentum of Richard's sword brought it crashing down, its blade sinking into the earth. In that second, Henry swung his sword in a mighty arc in a sideways move, the edge of his sword smashing into the elbow of Richard's sword arm, crumpling the elbow guard beneath it and driving it into the flesh of Richard's arm.

Richard let out a yell of pain, which was cut short as Henry let fly with his sword again, this time catching Richard high on the chest.

Richard tottered backward, then fell, dragged down by his armor.

The crown fell off his helmet and rolled into the mud.

Instantly, Henry snatched it up and held it aloft for all to see.

"Richard is dead!" he roared.

All those within earshot turned on hearing this.

Then they saw the figure of Richard, his armor now covered in mud, struggling to get up.

"The King lives!" shouted one of Richard's soldiers.

Henry put the crown on his own helmet, turned to tower over Richard, raising his sword, and then he brought it down in one hard crunching blow, and Richard lay still.

Henry waited for Richard to move again, but there came no movement.

By now a stillness had descended on the battle. The clanging of metal against metal had ceased.

Now, Henry lifted the crown from his helmet and held it up.

"Salute your King!" he shouted.

And one by one the soldiers, those that were Henry's and those who had been Richard's, fell to their knees, and the cry went up across the battlefield:

"Long live King Henry!"

RATINGS:
Knights in Armor

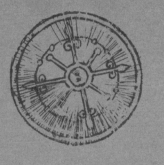

CODE OF HONOR: 5

RUTHLESSNESS: 6

WEAPONRY: 3

TACTICS: 3

COURAGE: 5

TOTAL: 22 **points**

4 TEXAS: THE ALAMO

The American Wild West was a vast sprawling area that attracted more and more settlers. It bred many legendary warriors: Native Americans such as Geronimo and Sitting Bull. Lawmen like Wyatt Earp and Wild Bill Hickok. Outlaws like Jesse James and Billy the Kid. Many of these were warriors for personal reasons: often revenge or money.

In the early nineteenth century, Texas was still part of Mexico. By 1830, large parts of Texas had been settled by many ranchers and hunters, most of them from America or Britain. A large number of these Texians, as they were called, wanted to be independent of Mexico.

THE WARRIORS

These people are all real historical figures:

William B. Travis. Just 27 years old at the time of the Alamo, Travis – a former lawyer – was the Commander of the Alamo during the siege by the Mexican army.

Davy Crockett. Famous as a frontiersman, he had also been elected to the American Congress and was considered by many as a potential President of America.

Jim Bowie. A formidable fighter, he is better known for his famous knife, "The Bowie Knife," which he used both for hunting and when fighting. This knife was actually created by Jim Bowie's brother, Rezin Bowie. Jim Bowie was also known to be a slave trader, a gambler, and often in debt.

General Santa Anna, or Antonio Lopez de Santa Anna Perez de Lebron, to give him his full name. Santa Anna made his way up through the ranks of the Mexican army as a soldier, serving with distinction during the Mexican Revolution of 1810-1812. Santa Anna was among those who urged Independence from Spain, and in 1821 – at the age of 27 – Santa Anna had taken command of the army and declared Mexico a Republic.

THE HARDWARE

CANNONS

THE ALAMO:

It is believed there were between eighteen and twenty-one serviceable cannons in the defense of the Alamo. These ranged from **4-pounders** to one enormous **18-pounder**.

Because of a lack of cannon balls, the gunners used pieces of scrap metal, cut-up bits of chain, and even broken horseshoes as ammunition.

THE MEXICAN ARMY:

It is believed the Mexican army used eight cannons against the Alamo during the siege: **two 8-pounders; two 6-pounders; two 4-pounders; and two 7" howitzers.**

MUSKETS

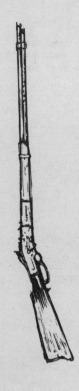

Used by both sides. Single-round long-barreled weapons. Highly inaccurate and of very short range. Because of a lack of ammunition, the defenders of the Alamo made their own musket balls, using lead from the chapel windows.

RIFLES

The Mexican army, as well as being equipped with muskets, also had surplus firearms from the British army, including the Baker Rifle. The Baker Rifle had a firing rate twice that of other military and hunting rifles of the time.

THE ALAMO: 1836 A.D.

The history behind the story

In 1835, the American settlers rose in revolt against the Mexican Government, demanding independence for Texas. The Mexican Government responded by sending its army to put down the rebellion.

The spirit of the rebellion was best seen at the building called the Mission of San Antonio de Valero, better known as the Alamo, in Texas, where about 190 rebels under the command of William B. Travis gathered together in 1836 to resist the might of the Mexican Army. The courage of these defenders who died for what they believed in is forever remembered with the rallying cry "Remember the Alamo!" to encourage future generations of Americans to fight for freedom at all costs.

This is a fictionalized story based on real events and real people.

M arch 5, 1836. From the journal of William B. Travis.

We have been under siege here for ten days now. There are 190 of us. Outside, surrounding us on all sides, is the Mexican army, which Crockett calculates to be about 3,000 strong. At least Santa Anna allowed most of the women and children to leave a few days ago. I pray to God they reached the town unharmed and will carry the message of what happened to us, if we do not survive. It does not look as if our reinforcements will arrive. There has been no word from Sam Houston. I believe he will let the Alamo fall rather than risk his own troops. Fannin, also, refuses to come from Goliad. He sends word that his men are poorly armed and tired. No more so than we.

Jim Bowie is sick and in bed. I believe he has pneumonia, or worse. I do not believe he will survive the sickness even if we win.

Travis laid down his pen and re-read his words. "*Even if we win,*" he mused bitterly. 190 against an army of 3,000. We have no real ammunition for our cannons. Hardly any ammunition for our muskets. Our food will run out in a few days. No one is going to come to our aid. And Santa Anna has given us a simple choice: unconditional surrender or die.

Travis dried the ink on the page carefully and then closed his journal and put it back in the drawer of his

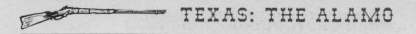

desk. He would rather live in an independent Texas, but if he were to die for one, so be it. There would be no surrender at the Alamo.

He checked his watch. Three o'clock. Time to check the afternoon watch. Military discipline had to be maintained. He believed it was only the discipline that was holding the men's morale together.

Travis stepped out of the cooling shadows of the clay-constructed building and into the harsh afternoon sunlight that bleached the inner courtyard of the mission. Around him were all the signs of the siege: holes in buildings where the Mexican cannonballs had crashed into them; broken timbers from the same attacks.

Travis looked up at the men keeping watch on the wooden platforms near the top of the Alamo's exterior walls. Most of them were the Tennesseeans who had come to the Alamo with Davy Crockett. Backwoodsmen. Hunters. Fur traders. Travis saw that the huge figure of Crockett himself was up there with them.

"Colonel Crockett!" called Travis. "What news?!"

Crockett looked down from the platform at Travis and grinned.

"Mexicans are still out there, Colonel Travis," he said. "If you were hoping they'd sneak off, no luck there."

"Keep me informed, Colonel," nodded Travis. With that he saluted and went off to make further checks on the sentries posted around the outer walls of the Alamo.

Sam Blair, one of Davy Crockett's oldest friends, chewed on his plug of black tobacco, spat, then looked after the departing Travis and shook his head.

"All this 'Colonel' business," he sighed. "Does Travis

think we're in the army, Davy?"

"Guess we are, Sam," shrugged Crockett. "The Army of the Republic of Texas."

"Dang me," grunted Sam. "My ma always said to me 'Don't never get caught up with no army, Samuel. You'll only find yourself in trouble.'"

Crockett looked out at the lines of thousands and thousands of Mexican soldiers, all at a safe distance from the Alamo.

"Looks like your ma was right," he said ruefully.

"What I can't understand is why they don't just come at us and get it over with?" grumbled Sam.

In the hastily improvised medical room, Jim Bowie was lying on a straw mattress on a low wooden cot. As he walked in, Travis saw at once that Bowie's condition had worsened. Bowie's clothes were almost black with sweat, and his face glistened with beads of perspiration. Bowie shook and groaned and muttered. His eyes were closed.

Travis looked at Stephen Dennison, who was acting as the Alamo's doctor.

"How is he, Mr. Dennison?" he asked.

"Feverish," said Dennison. "I can't do anything for him except keep him cool with water. But with this siege, water could be in short supply. There's no telling how long the well will last."

"Do your best, Mr. Dennison," said Travis.

Suddenly Bowie's eyes opened and he jerked up and then supported himself on one elbow. For an instant the cloudiness over his eyes seemed to clear, then it came back again.

"Travis," he gasped, his voice hoarse and rasping. "Is

82

that you? I can't see."

"It's me, Colonel Bowie," said Travis.

"What's happening? Have the Mexicans attacked?"

"Not yet," said Travis. "I think they're hoping we'll surrender."

"No surrender!" croaked Bowie. "Never surrender!"

And then his body became wracked with a fit of coughing, and he slumped back down on the soaking wet straw mattress.

"Don't worry, there will be no surrender," said Travis. "We'll show both General Santa Anna and our fellow Americans what Texians are made of."

But Bowie's eyes had closed and he had fallen back into a fitful broken sleep.

"If we can't get him to a doctor soon, I believe he will die, Colonel," said Dennison. "In fact, I'm surprised he's lasted as long as he has, considering his condition."

"Colonel Bowie has an iron will and an iron constitution," said Travis. "He's pulled through worse situations than this."

"I still believe he will die in the next few days, Colonel," said Dennison, dropping his voice to a whisper in case Bowie could hear.

Travis was on the point of responding, "We're all going to die in the next few days," but he checked himself. While there was life there was hope. And maybe he was wrong. Maybe Houston would arrive with reinforcements. Or Fannin. Whatever, it wouldn't do to lower morale. The men had to think there was a chance of winning.

Beyond the walls, out on the arid Texan plain that surrounded the tiny mission that was the Alamo, Santa Anna sat in his tent in conference with his second-in-command, Vicente Filisola.

"Well?" he demanded. "What is our intelligence? Are reinforcements on their way?"

Filisola shook his head.

"We have intercepted messengers, both from Houston and from Fannin at Goliad. Fannin is coming with 400 men. Houston is staying away."

Santa Anna thought this over.

"And when will Fannin get here?"

"Goliad is a hundred miles away. He will have set off a day ago. He will be here in two days at the most."

"400 hundred men are nothing against our army, but they could create problems for us if we are attacking the Alamo when they arrive." Santa Anna studied the plan of the Alamo on his makeshift table: the known locations of the Alamo's defensive cannons; the placing of his own troops and his own artillery. He reached a decision.

"We will attack at dawn tomorrow," he announced firmly.

March 6, 1836. Dawn.

5:00 A.M. On the wooden platform just inside the north-west corner of the Alamo's outer wall, the three Texian sentries on watch scanned the Mexican lines. They were almost dropping with tiredness. Their eyes were strained from peering out at the waiting Mexican army throughout the long hours of darkness.

Suddenly there was a movement among the Mexican lines about 300 yards away. Something was happening. A long wooden ladder could be seen, held by some of the Mexican soldiers. Then another ladder.

Suddenly the sentries heard a cry from the Mexican front line in Spanish: "Adelante!" Forward! Immediately the sound of bugles could be heard, then another cry: "Arriba!!" Attack!!

As the sentries watched, the Mexican soldiers broke into a run toward the walls of the Alamo, firing their muskets, then reloading and running onward. From the wooden platform the alarm went up: "The Mexicans are coming!!"

Inside the Alamo, men tumbled out of their beds or roused themselves from the earth floors where they had been sleeping, snatching up their muskets as they ran.

On the wooden platform the sentries were already firing at the oncoming Mexicans, but it was like firing into an army of rushing ants. As fast as each musket was fired, by the time it had been primed, re-powdered, reloaded, and was ready to fire again, the advancing Mexicans had made it to the foot of the wall.

The Texians, now fully awake, clambered up the wooden steps and on to the wooden platform atop the wall to give support to their comrades, their muskets adding to the deafening fusillade.

The ladders were now leaning against the walls of the Alamo. The defenders hacked at the tops of the ladders with hand axes and with the butts of their muskets, trying to break them and dislodge them, but the Mexicans were clambering up thick and fast. As one Mexican fell dead and tumbled back to the ground, another was coming behind.

Travis rushed to his post in the northwest corner. As he mounted the wooden platform at the top of the wall he could see the tops of the scaling ladders resting against the wall. He hurried to the wall, his shotgun ready, and fired downward. Screams from below told him he had hit his target.

He was breaking open his shotgun to reload when he felt a sharp blow hit him full in the forehead. I am hit, he thought, and then he felt himself falling falling falling . . .

"Travis is killed!" Sam Burns shouted at Davy Crockett.

"What?! How? When?"

Crockett leveled his musket, Old Betsy, at the Mexicans struggling up the ladder and fired. Boom!! The leading Mexicans tumbled down, but more were coming up.

"George Taylor saw him go down," said Burns. "He took a musket ball in the head."

Crockett battled to reload his musket, then gave up in disgust. There was no time for this. Reversing his musket and holding it by the barrel, he began to wield it as a club. If he could just keep them from getting over the wall . . .

All around the Alamo the Mexicans were attacking, coming in over the tops of the walls, pouring in through cracks in the walls where the Mexican cannon had smashed the Alamo defenses during the siege.

The defenders on the platform on the walls now found themselves attacked on all sides as the Mexicans fought their way into the main courtyard of the mission. The dawn air was thick with the smell of burnt gunpowder as musket after musket was fired until the barrels were too hot to fire.

"Take cover inside!!" roared Crockett.

Fighting every inch of the way, the defenders now abandoned the platforms and made for the Alamo buildings. They had prepared these during the ten days of the siege: strengthening the doors, setting up barricades of sand and clay inside the walls, ensuring that the windows were wide enough to fire out but too narrow for the enemy to get a good shot in.

The Mexicans were now well inside the outer walls of the mission. The gates had been opened and the bulk of the Mexican army was now pouring in.

From his position inside the hospital, Stephen Dennison looked out through the narrow window and saw a large cannon being hauled in through the open main gates.

On the bed, Jim Bowie roused himself, forcing himself up, and then fell back again.

"Mexicans?" he gasped, fighting for air.

Dennison nodded.

"Give me my gun," said Bowie.

"They might spare you if they see you are ill . . ." began Dennison, but Bowie cut him short. "I ain't got the breath to argue," he wheezed painfully. "Give me my gun."

Dennison hesitated, then lifted Bowie's pistol from the table and handed it to the dying man. As he did so, the door of the room crashed in and a dozen Mexican soldiers spilled into the room, rifles with bayonets attached at the ready.

"For Texas!" Bowie roared hoarsely and struggled to aim his pistol. He never made it. A volley of rifle fire burst out and Jim Bowie fell back onto the straw mattress, dead.

Dennison threw himself at the attackers, but the Mexican

bayonets flashed in the sunlight that was coming in through the window and Dennison went down.

Inside the building that acted as the food store, Davy Crockett and some of his fellow Tennesseeans were holed up, firing out through the narrow windows.

"Looks like we've got trouble, Davy," grunted John Hayes.

"More than we got already?" asked Crockett sarcastically.

"Guess so," said Hayes. "The Mexes have brought themselves a cannon up and looks like they're gonna blow the door in. And maybe this building with it."

Crockett looked out through the narrow window. What Hayes said was true. The cannon was lined up and the Mexican soldiers were already loading a huge heavy cannonball into its muzzle.

"Shucks!!" spat Crockett. "Well, I never did like being stuck indoors, anyhow. What say we go outside and get this over with?"

"I'm with you, Davy," nodded Hayes. "I never did want to die indoors."

"Okay, get that door open and let's get out there!"

The Tennesseeans heaved up the bar that barricaded the door, and they pulled it open.

The Mexicans manning the cannon turned, surprised. And then Davy Crockett and his fellow Tennesseeans were running at them, their backwoods hunting knives in their hands.

"For Tennessee and Texas, boys!" yelled Crockett.

And then they were engulfed in a sea of Mexican uniforms. But as they went down, they were still fighting.

From his position outside the Alamo, Santa Anna

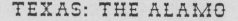

watched. The sound of firing from inside the mission was growing more sporadic. He checked his watch. Nearly 7 o'clock. Just two hours since the siege had begun, and the Alamo had fallen.

Santa Anna smiled to himself as he mounted his horse. They were all dead, of that he was sure. He himself had given the orders: take no prisoners. All those rebels, those famous names, Travis, Bowie, Crockett, and the others, all dead. Finished. The Texian rebellion was over. Yes, he thought to himself as he trotted his horse toward the smoldering ruin, his senior officers by his side, when this day is remembered, people will honor the name of Antonio Lopez de Santa Anna Perez de Lebron and say proudly, "Remember the Alamo!"

RATINGS:

TEXAN DEFENDERS

CODE OF HONOR: 10

RUTHLESSNESS: 7

WEAPONRY: 3

TACTICS: 4

COURAGE: 10

TOTAL: 34 points

5 U.S. SPECIAL FORCES

U.S. Special Forces teams are usually either 6-man or 12-man. A 6-man team consists of a Team Leader, the Assistant Team Leader, who also doubles as a radio operator, and ideally at least one person able to act as an interpreter in local situations. In many war situations they operate covertly behind enemy lines.

THE HARDWARE

Each member of a team would normally carry the following:

First aid packet – including morphine syrettes in a crush-proof box

Four canteens for water, with purification tablets

Smoke for signaling

Compass

Small survival kit

Signal mirror

Weapon cleaning equipment

Inspect repellent

Emergency rations

Knife

Flare gun with 4 – 6 flares

4 – 6 ammo pouches

Fragmentation grenades

Assault rifle

WEAPONS

M16A2 – an upgraded version of the original classic M16. A high-velocity assault rifle. Weighs 3.85 kg (8 lb 8 oz). The magazine contains 30 rounds. Has a cyclic rate of fire of 600 rounds per minute.

203 – An M16
Armalite rifle with a
grenade launcher
attached. This fires a
40mm bomb.

Brunswick RAW – a device fitted to a
standard M16 assault rifle. It fires a
sphere containing 1.27 kilograms of high
explosive that has high impact against
light armored vehicles. It can
also blow a hole 300 mm
across in 200 mm-thick
reinforced concrete. Its
effective range is about 200
meters (220 yards).

Iraqi Scud missiles: The Russian-built SS-
IC Scud-B has a range of 100-175 miles. It
is 37 feet long and 3 feet wide. As well as
using conventional high explosives, the
warheads can also contain nuclear,
biological, or chemical material.

Mobile Scuds
used by the Iraqi army
were carried on an
8-wheeled transporter,
which also acted as a
launcher for the rockets.

U.S. SPECIAL FORCES: THE GULF WAR, 1991

The history behind the story

On August 2, 1990, Saddam Hussein's Iraqi forces invaded Kuwait. Outraged at this attack on a small nation, and also aware that if Saddam held control of Kuwait it would give the Iraqi dictator control of much of the world's reserves of oil, a Coalition force led by the USA, Saudi Arabia, and Britain assembled in Saudi Arabia, prepared to drive the Iraqi forces out of Kuwait.

In December 1990, Saddam launched long-range Scud missile attacks on Israel from positions in the west of Iraq, hitting civilian targets in Tel Aviv. Saddam's hope was that Israel would retaliate and enter the war. The Allies were concerned that if that happened, then the Arab nations would feel forced to support Iraq against Israel. Iran might even join the war on Iraq's side. It was vitally important that the Scud attacks on Israel be stopped.

Allied airpower was concentrated on the known bases where the Scud missiles aimed at Israel were fired from, and most of these were soon put out of action. However, many Scuds were being fired from mobile launchers. These had to be taken out, and fast. There was only one answer and that was for Allied Special Forces – U.S. Special Forces and the British SAS – to be deployed behind enemy lines: to penetrate deep into Iraqi territory, find the mobile Scud launchers, and destroy them. This is a fictionalized account of one such mission.

The helicopter hadn't even touched down onto the desert floor when the six men began leaping out of the opening in its side, dropping down and rolling to soften their landing. The whole time their rifles were in their hands, ready to use. In the darkness the only sound they could hear was the deafening battering of the helicopter's rotor blades.

The helicopter pilot paused just long enough to check that all six men were out and their equipment with them, and then the helicopter soared upward and vanished into the black night sky.

The sky was clear, filled with stars. Here, deep inside Iraq, all around them was the flatness of the desert, with occasional rises of a wadi. It was cold. In the desert during the day you can burn, at night you can freeze to death.

In theory the men knew where they were. They had studied the maps and the reconnaissance photographs. But all of them knew that there was a big difference between what the maps and the photos said and the reality on the ground.

Captain Chuck Phillips gestured to the patrol to fan out, check that the area was secure. All this was done in absolute silence, no talking. The noise of the helicopter coming down and then rising and vanishing could have been explained to any Iraqi living out here as just a reconnaissance flight. Normal in times in war. People speaking in English was another matter.

The six men soon regrouped. Using night vision, they had scanned to the horizon.

"All clear, Cap," whispered Matt Davis, the Assistant Team Leader.

On any mission like this behind enemy lines, the men talked in whispers. It was a habit that often saved lives. Sounds carried, and the enemy could be anywhere.

Chuck nodded.

"Okay," he said.

He checked the map.

According to Intelligence, the Iraqis transported their Scuds along an MSR, a Main Supply Route, that ran northeast to southwest from Baghdad to Amman. Top Brass called this whole area where the Scuds were being fired from The Scud Box and had split it into two sections: Scud Boulevard, to the north of the MSR, and Scud Alley, to the south. U.S. Special Forces were designated into Scud Boulevard and the British SAS were operating in the southern part of the MSR.

It made sense, cutting out the unlucky chance of a "blue-on-blue": one outfit accidentally firing on the other. Both Special Forces tended to shoot first and ask questions afterward.

Chuck followed the line of the MSR on his map. The route ran straight across the desert for miles and miles, with just a few bends where the road was forced to bypass rocky hills.

"What's the plan, Cap?" asked Danny Roberts.

There had been many plans talked about back at base: the best way to take out a mobile Scud launcher and its crew. Chuck remembered what they had been told about the mobile Scuds:

Scuds were carried on a mobile launcher, known as a TEL (transporter erector launcher). The TEL had a crew of three: two in the front and the third in the back. Plus, there would be vehicles with infantry support.

In charge of the convoy would be a command vehicle, possibly a Land Cruiser. This would carry the commander of the team and a surveyor. According to Intelligence, the surveyor was the key man in the team. Once the Scud team arrived at their chosen site, accurate site-surveying had to be carried out before the Scud could be launched. Upper-atmosphere balloons had to be tracked by radar and the angle of deflection had to be calculated, all the work of the surveyor.

While the surveyor was doing all this, the propellants had to be pumped into the missiles and the coordinates of the target tapped in by the launch operator. It was reckoned that all this would take about an hour. Intelligence had suggested that while these preparations were going on would be the best time to hit the Scud teams, while they were stationary. Chuck thought that there were many problems with Intelligence's suggestion:

One: the Special Forces team were on foot. Once they had spotted the Scud convoy, how did they follow them across open desert?

Two: Before the Scud team started carrying out their operations, it was fairly certain that their infantry support would have set up a defensive perimeter around the site. This would have to be broken through first before they got to the TEL.

No, Chuck had other ideas. He tapped one of the bends on the MSR on the map.

"Here's where we hit 'em," he said. "The convoy will have to slow down for a bend."

"These are Iraqi troops," put in Garcia Perez. "They

don't have to slow down for anything. Goat-herders, goats, whatever, anyone coming around that bend the other way gets out of the way or gets run over. They don't care."

"They care about rolling a vehicle and dropping a Scud," grinned Chuck. "Believe me, they'll slow down just because they have to. And when a convoy takes a bend, they're broken up and out of sight of each other; even just a second is long enough."

The others nodded in agreement. What Chuck said made sense.

"We'll pick one of these where the road bends to the left," Chuck continued. "That means the rocks will also be on the left, where we'll take cover. Because, if our Intelligence is correct, the door to the command-post of the TEL is in the center of the vehicle, with its door on the left-hand side. That's our main target."

"What about taking out the missile, Cap?" asked Danny.

Chuck gave a slight smile.

"The missile warhead could contain chemicals or biological weapons. It might even have a nuke warhead. If that goes up when we're around it, it's goodbye and amen, fellas," he said quietly. "No, the Top Brass will want us to do this again, which means we stay alive, if we can. So we knock out the TEL and leave it stranded. Take out as many of the enemy as we can, then radio for air support to get us out of here, and leave it to the Air Force to take out the Scud and the rest of Scud crew. You okay with that?"

The other five nodded.

"Okay," said Chuck. "Let's get moving. We need to be in place before dawn."

The six men made good time across the desert, despite the weight of their equipment. Faster than Chuck had expected. They were helped because here the ground was hard rock, not soft shifting sand. And it was flat. On the downside, this posed a problem because if they should come up against the enemy, there was nowhere for them to take cover. The few ridges and holes in the rocks weren't deep enough to give proper protection.

Luckily, at this time of night, the locals were safely indoors. No one tended goats in the middle of the night.

The six – Chuck Phillips, Matt Davis, Danny Roberts, Garcia Perez, Karl Mannheim, and Otis Pearce, the youngest of the team – navigated by bearings and distance. They had a Global Positioning System, but Chuck was wary about using it in case the signals were picked up by enemy satellite watchers. Also, when used, the machinery gave off light. Faint light, but out here in the blackness of the desert night even the faintest light could be picked up by a careful observer. Chuck had been assured the GPS was foolproof, but too often in the past Chuck had known gadgets that were deemed foolproof in the lab to cause problems on the ground, and he was taking no chances on this mission. This caution was one of the reasons why Chuck had wanted the team set down at a distance from the MSR rather than right on it. If any Iraqi patrols had been traveling the MSR at night, reports of a helicopter on the MSR could have warned the enemy and blown the whole mission. Safer to land away from the ambush site and walk to it.

They located the MSR at 0400, 90 minutes before dawn. They could tell it was the MSR by the well-worn marks of heavy vehicles going in both directions. The rock formation marked the bend.

"Score one for navigation," reflected Chuck with relief.

The rock formation was almost a small hill. Chuck hoped it was large enough to find cover in. The problem was the lack of vegetation. It would be a case of finding holes in the rock and digging in. Not too high up the rock, because if the enemy starting bombarding the rocks with heavy artillery, they had to be able to get away from the line of fire. But also not too low down, because they needed to get an overview of the approaching convoy.

"Okay. Take positions," said Chuck. "Make sure you're in visual contact with each other. The target should be coming from the northeast, so that's where I, Matt, Danny, and Garcia will be aiming. Karl and Otis, start by taking the other side of the hill, just in case the enemy launches a counterattack from that direction. Okay, let's go."

The six men hauled themselves up the rocks, looking for the best place to find cover that would keep them out of sight of the Iraqis. And that included any casual local who might be passing.

Weapons were put in position, aimed toward the tracks where previous heavy vehicles had passed.

On Chuck's instructions, Matt radioed their position.

One of the AWACs would pick it up and mark it, ready for action. When they sent for back-up to pull them out after the ambush, they'd need it in a hurry.

Chuck set out the order of ambush:

"Danny, you're using the Brunswick. Take out the command post in the middle of the TEL. Matt, hit the cab of the TEL with a 203, that should knock it dead. I'll use a 203 as well and take out the next important target. Everyone else, hit any aerials you can see and knock out their chances of radioing for help. The last thing we want is the Iraqi air force turning up and blasting us."

Although Chuck knew that most of the Iraqi air force was being kept out of the skies by the Allied planes, there was no knowing when an Iraqi gunship might be mobilized.

Then the waiting began.

For the men, this was the worst part. You set an ambush and waited and hoped your target would come along. And sooner rather than later. Waiting like this could often take hours. Sometimes even days. Chuck remembered when he and Danny had once set up an ambush in the jungle and had waited four days before their target arrived. Four days of insects, heat, sweat, and staying alert, waiting.

Dawn came, and the desert landscape came properly to light. Bare rocks for as far as the eye could see.

Now they could see the MSR fully. It wasn't a proper road as such, just the marks of vehicles in the rocky dust of the desert floor. At this point Chuck guessed the trackway was about 300 meters wide. He hoped the Iraqis wouldn't be traveling on the far side of the track, away from their cover point. The Brunswick had an effective range of 200 meters. They needed the TEL to be inside that range for their firepower to have the full effect.

Time passed. Minutes stretching into an hour. Then two hours. The sun was scorching down on them now and they huddled into their rocks, their faces protected from the sun's glare by their combat headgear. Still there was no movement in the desert. And then they saw it. In the distance, coming from the northeast. A cloud of dust. Vehicles.

"This is it," muttered Chuck. "Fire on my command."

The men pushed themselves down into the rock as far as they could. They hoped the tape covering their assault rifles would hide any reflection from the sun's rays.

Danny had the round bomb already fixed to his M16, and Matt had turned his assault rifle into a 203. They were ready.

The dust cloud came nearer, and now they could hear the sounds of the heavy vehicles.

Chuck trained his binoculars on the approaching vehicles. It was a TEL all right. He could make out the Scud missile on its staging at the back of the long vehicle. Immediately in front of the TEL, leading the convoy, was an armored car. Behind the TEL came an armored Land Cruiser, which Chuck guessed held the commander and the surveyor. Bringing up the rear was an open truck carrying about twenty armed Iraqi soldiers.

Chuck did a swift calculation. Twenty soldiers in the truck, two in the cab, three in the TEL, say four in the Land Cruiser, and another four in the armored car. Thirty-three against their six. The team would have to make sure their opening fire took out as many of the enemy as possible before they had a chance to counterattack.

The convoy was getting nearer

Chuck weighed up which target he should aim his 203 at, the lead armored car or the Land Cruiser command vehicle. Logic said to hit the Land Cruiser and take out the commander of the convoy, but that would leave the leading vehicle untouched.

But not for long, Chuck thought grimly. He'd take the Land Cruiser out first and then turn his attention to the armored car.

The convoy was almost upon their position now. Five hundred meters. Four. Three. Two. One hundred.

"Go!" barked Chuck.

Matt's round from his 203 tore into the radiator of the TEL, tearing the engine apart and exploding in the cab. The TEL bucked like a horse, and as it did Danny let fly with the Brunswick, his round ripping through the steel door and smashing into the TEL's command post.

At the same time, Chuck sent his missile in through the windshield of the Land Cruiser and saw the vehicle explode, hot metal flying in all directions.

The armored car in the lead braked to a screeching halt and began to turn, aiming at the rocks so that its guns could get a fix. Chuck hurled a grenade so that it bounced just in front of the armored car and then rolled under it. The force of the explosion threw the armored car up, and then it sank down on its buckled axles.

Meanwhile, Karl, Garcia, and Otis were hammering round after round into the open truck as the Iraqi soldiers in the back tried to jump clear.

The driver of the truck, seeing that the track ahead was obstructed, threw the vehicle into reverse and tried to spin it around and head back the way he'd come. This sudden jolting action only threw the Iraqi soldiers still in the truck off balance. A burst of fire from Otis took out the truck's side tires, and it ground to a halt.

Many of the soldiers had survived and they now scrambled for cover behind the disabled truck.

Other soldiers were spilling out of the wreck of the armored car, their guns blazing at the rocks where the Special Forces team were in cover. There was no sign of life from the TEL or the command Land Cruiser.

"Okay, time to get the hell out of here," said Chuck. "Matt, tell the cavalry they can come in any time."

Matt hit the radio. Because of the deafening gunfire Chuck couldn't hear what Matt was saying, but he guessed he was calling in air support. Chuck hoped the Air Force back-up wasn't too far away.

The Iraqi soldiers were blazing away now, their gunfire smashing into the rocks in front of and behind the team's position. Chuck wondered if the Iraqis had managed to get a message out for help. If they had, it would be a case of who got to them first.

The Scud missile was still on its launch pad on the back of the TEL. The front of the TEL was twisted and still burning.

"Incoming!" yelled Karl.

Chuck looked at the direction where Karl was pointing. Helicopters, three of them. Ours or theirs? he wondered.

As the helicopters drew nearer he recognized the

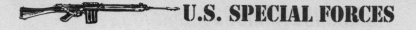

shapes. They're our boys! he sighed with relief. Two gunships and a Chinook.

The two gunships began strafing the Iraqis sheltering behind the wrecked and smoldering vehicles. The Chinook swooped over the team's position and began to come down at a position on the far side of the rocks from the MSR and the scene of the ambush.

"Okay, boys, the taxi's here!" yelled Chuck. "Go go go!"

While the two gunships carried on the battle with the Iraqis, the six Special Forces men took advantage of this covering fire to scramble down from their positions on the rocks. They hit the floor of the desert and then headed as fast as they could for the waiting Chinook, taking turns to turn and give covering fire at their rear.

They scrambled aboard the Chinook, and then the helicopter lifted up and they were airborne.

"The Scud!" shouted Chuck to the pilot.

"It's being dealt with," came the reply.

Chuck looked out of the helicopter back at the scene of the ambush at the vehicles still burning, and, as he watched, a missile from one of the gunships tore into the Scud.

There was an enormous explosion that completely blotted out their view of the desert as the Scud missile disintegrated.

The Chinook soared up higher and then accelerated away, heading for the safety of the Saudi border.

Chuck and the other five of his patrol exchanged grins. One Scud missile less. One Scud mobile launcher less. Mission accomplished.

RATINGS:
U.S. SPECIAL FORCES

CODE OF HONOR: **8**

RUTHLESSNESS: **9**

WEAPONRY: **10**

TACTICS: **7**

COURAGE: **10**

TOTAL: **44** POINTS

6 ROBOT WARS

Already robots do many things. They build our cars. They can operate farther out in space and go deeper beneath the oceans than humans are capable of. They can be as big as a whole space station, or as small as the minutest piece of nanotechnology, to carry out surgical repairs inside a human body in places too microscopic for a human to handle.

Many wars are now being fought by robots: robot tanks, unmanned aircraft. Decisions are being made directly by computers. Developments in A.I. (artificial intelligence) could lead to intelligent robots becoming the most powerful weapons of all.

THE HARDWARE

Cyber-Warrior: Constructed with:

– Brain-to-machine communication: A microchip made from DNA grown in the human brain, allowing the brain to be used as a remote control mechanism to activate weapons by thought

– Skeleton replaced with strong hi-tech components

– Synthetic muscle tissue resistant to damage

– Cloning for spare body parts to repair or replace damage to Cyber-Warrior's organic components

– Electronically enhanced senses (e.g. hearing, eyesight)

A.I. Robot Machines

Self-controlled missiles with on-board computers to navigate through enemy defenses

Defensive protective laser shield

"Invisibility" cloaking device to avoid being targeted

Homing device for pinpointing weapons to specific target

Robot Wars – 2099 A.D.

The history behind the story

By the year 2075, a combination of genetic engineering and hi-tech advances had produced The Warrior: a human with specially strengthened muscles and bones and a microchip grown from human DNA at the base of the brain that gave The Warrior direct mind-to-machine contact. This meant that a Warrior flying an attack plane simply had to think "fire missiles!" and the ship's missiles would fire.

By 2090, new advances in robot technology made these genetically engineered Warriors obsolete; all warplanes and war machinery were now operated by robots controlled from a distance by computers.

Then, in 2099, a new threat came to Earth, this one from deep in Outer Space: intelligent robotic forms, who launched a sudden and terrifying attack on Earth.

CRASHHHHHHH!!!!!!!!!!!!!!!!!!
KABOOOOOOOOOOM!!!!!!!!!!!!!

Even here, in the Space Control Center in Arizona, deep below the earth's surface, the effects of the bombardment could be felt. The whole Control Center rocked as more missiles smashed into the flat areas of desert above it.

"I believe they're deliberately targeting our position, General!" Professor Linda Myers said, scanning the readouts on the screen in front of her.

Next to her, General Mike Moffat nodded.

"How come they know so much about us? Where our base is?" he demanded.

"They're robots," pointed out Myers. "They don't need eyes, or spies, or anything, just good hi-tech equipment. And if they got all the way here from halfway across space, scanning us is child's play to them."

SMASHHH!!!!!!!!!!!!

Once again, the Control Center rocked. This time there was a flash of sparks from one of the banks of monitors in one corner of the enormous control room.

Automatically, the fire protection system kicked in, smothering the sparks with a blanket of foam before they could turn into flames.

"Controls for the life-support systems have been hit, General!" called a technician. "Our air supply has been compromised!"

"Okay, bring the back-up system on line!" ordered the General.

Turning back to Myers, he demanded, "How are these things getting through? What's happened to our defenses? Why aren't our robot ships taking them out?"

"Because they *are* robot ships, I'm afraid, General," sighed Myers. "These alien ships have set up some kind of force field around them that our robot ships can't penetrate. The aliens are sending messages to our robot ships that deflect them back toward us. To be honest, we've been lucky that our own ships haven't attacked *us* so far. But if this goes on, we could soon be shooting down our own ships as well as trying to defend ourselves against these alien robots."

KERPOOWWW!!!!! BAMMMMMMMM!!!!!!!!!

Once more the Control Center shuddered, and this time a whole row of monitors shut down, the screens going blank.

"They're cutting off our control of our own ships!" called one of the operators.

The General groaned.

"There has to be *something* we can do!"

Myers hesitated, then she said: "There is one chance."

"Anything!" said the General, grabbing at any possibility.

"We could try re-activating The Warriors."

"The Warriors?!" The General stared at her. "Are you kidding? They all got laid out to grass years ago! None of them have seen active service for I don't know how long! That's if any of them are even still alive."

"I know a couple who are still around," said Myers.

"A couple!" snorted the General. "What chance does that give us against this kind of enemy?!"

"They may be the only chance we've got," Myers pointed out.

Once again heavy missiles struck the Arizona desert far above them, and a deep thud went through the Control Center. All the lights went out momentarily, flicking back in at a lower intensity as the emergency lighting came on. This time both the General and Myers saw that part of the ceiling had come down, smoke and dust were billowing toward them. They both choked and frantically covered their mouths and noses.

"Okay!" coughed the General. "Get out there and find your Warriors. But if they're our best hope, then God help us!"

Buzz Walton sat in his lounge and watched the War on his TV. On every channel were the images of the bombardment, which seemed to be coming from just outside the earth's atmosphere. So far the attacks appeared to be concentrated on the earth's larger cities: New York, London, Moscow, Hong Kong. Out here in North Dakota, almost to the Canadian border, they'd escaped the attacks from these aliens, whoever or whatever they were. Buzz's satellite dish meant he was able to pick up signals from almost anywhere, and the micro-chip in the base of his brain meant that it didn't matter if the newscast was in English, or Russian, or Chinese, or whatever language, he could switch to his translator mode and understand what was being said.

The thing that no one seemed to be saying was what lay behind these attacks. What did these aliens want? Who were they? Where were they from? There was plenty of guesswork, but no real answers.

The sound of his door chimes pulled his attention away from the newscast on the TV.

"Who is it?" he asked.

"A visitor," the robot voice of his door security system answered. "Female."

"Put her on the intercom," said Buzz.

There was a click as the security system connected Buzz to the door phone, then he asked:

"Who's calling and what do you want?"

"Linda Myers and I'm looking for a Warrior," came the voice. "Open this door, Buzz, and let me in. I've come a long way and I'm worn out. Air travel in a war zone isn't easy."

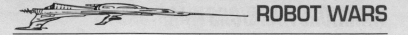

A few minutes later, Buzz and Myers were seated together in the lounge, Myers's fingers wrapped around a cup of coffee. The TV screen still flickered with its images of the War, though Buzz had now turned the sound to mute.

"You're looking for a Warrior, huh?" said Buzz.

Myers nodded.

Buzz shook his head ruefully.

"It's been a few long years since I've heard that word," said Buzz. "I thought we were obsolete. Put out of business by machines that did everything better." Pointedly, he added: "And if I remember rightly, you were the one who made those new and better machines, Professor."

Myers sipped at her coffee and nodded.

"You're right, Buzz," she said. "All I can say is, it seemed like a good idea at the time."

Buzz nodded toward the TV screen, where another city was shown being devastated by missiles, buildings burning and tumbling down, people running blindly in a doomed effort to try and escape the carnage.

"Until this," he said.

"Until this," nodded Myers in agreement.

"So, who are they, and what do they want?" he asked.

"We don't know," replied Myers. "There have been no demands for surrender. So, we guess they plan to just destroy us."

"And what would be the use of that? All they'd be left with would be a dead planet."

"Not quite," said Myers. "A planet without humans.

That's not quite the same thing."

"True," said Buzz. "So?"

"So, all we know about them is they're machines," said Myers. "They seem to have no organic life forms. What we're not sure is whether they're working for some other organic intelligence far away in space or whether they're just intelligent machines. A robot life form. Whatever it is, at the moment it's academic. We have to stop them, and none of our systems seem to be able to do that."

"None of your *robot* systems," countered Buzz.

"Exactly," agreed Myers. "Which is why we need to reactivate The Warriors."

"What makes you think we can stop these things if nothing else can?" asked Buzz. "Face it, we've all gotten older. None of us have been in action for nearly ten years, and that's a very long time."

"You had the best possible technology implanted. That should still be as quick as it ever was."

"As quick as these alien robots?" demanded Buzz.

"Buzz, let me lay it on the line. You're the only chance we've got. You and the other Warriors. If you guys can't stop these aliens, Earth is finished as far as we humans are concerned. Our robot ships can't break through whatever force fields these aliens have put around themselves. To get to them, we need some old-fashioned human cunning. We need something that acts like a machine but thinks like a human."

Buzz shrugged and gave a rueful grin.

"Okay," he said. "You've sold me. When do we start?"

The twelve Warriors were assembled in the underground briefing room. As Buzz Walton looked around the room, his mind went back to almost ten years ago and the last time the Warriors had been assembled together. At that time they were being told they were no longer needed, that they were being replaced by machines. At that time there had been about a hundred Warriors. He wondered what had happened to all those others in the years since?

Most of the other eleven he knew. He had fought side by side with them. Especially two of them, Chuck Mathews and Danny Garcia. The three of them had been inducted as Warriors at the same time. Trained together. Comrades in arms in the same unit.

He forced himself to turn back and pay attention to what General Moffat was saying.

The General was standing in front of a hologram of one of the alien robot fighter planes, pointing out how small it was.

"Our thinking is there's no way these craft could have made it all the way from deep space to Earth on their own," he said. "Even if they're not human, something this small will need technical back-up."

"Maybe they *are* their own technical back-up," put in

Mathews. "With nanotechnology anything is possible. They could create whatever they wanted right there up in space."

"What about ammunition?" asked the General.

"Same thing," said Mathews. "Nanotechnology."

"You still need the basic materials," pointed out Buzz.

"You can do it by assembling microbes," said Mathews.

As the others looked at him, Mathews shrugged apologetically.

"I did my Masters in nanotechnology," he explained.

"Even with nanotechnology, I still think the General's right about these things not having come here on their own," said Danny Garcia. "I reckon there's a mother ship up there somewhere."

"The trouble is, if there is, we can't see it," grunted the General. "These things are scrambling all our radar and satellite observation systems. We can't even pick these attack ships up until they're right in our face and start shooting missiles at us."

"So I guess that means we have to go up and take a closer look," said Buzz.

The General nodded.

"We're sending up four shuttles at dawn tomorrow. Each one will have three of you Warriors on board, with three space runabouts. We've adapted the runabouts, adding in weaponry, missiles, everything we could think of."

"Just twelve of us against these aliens?" asked Mathews.

"You're lucky there will be that many of you," said the

General. "With the damage we've taken since these attacks started, we've only got four shuttles left. We've stripped those and thrown out everything that isn't vital to survival to get the runabouts in as well as you guys. Tomorrow's shot is our last and only throw of the dice. Find that mother ship, destroy it, and knock out as many of these alien attack craft as you can. Otherwise, it's all over for us."

Buzz Walton, Chuck Mathews, and Danny Garcia lay strapped in their seats in their shuttle. Further along the launching pad, three other giant booster rockets, each with a shuttle atop, dominated the skyline.

"Fifteen seconds to launch," said. the voice in their headsets. "Fourteen, thirteen . . ."

In the control center, Linda Myers and General Moffat watched the countdown on the monitors. Twelve seconds to go, ten . . .

"What's that?!" came a shout of alarm.

They all looked and saw the horrifying sight of three alien robot fighters coming in, aiming directly at the rockets on their launch pads.

Nine seconds. Eight . . . .

BAMMMMOOOOOSHHHHH!!!!!!!!!!!!!!!

As the launch crew watched horrified, one of the rockets took a direct hit and erupted into a ball of rising flame.

"Abort the launch!" yelled one of the Mission Controllers, but the General's voice cut through the room with a sharp "No!"

The voice of the countdown continued: Seven, six, five, four . . .

"Those rockets and men are the only chance we have!" snapped the General.

On screen they could see that anti-aircraft batteries had opened up, trying to get a fix on the again incoming alien robot fighters, but they were having difficulty as the robot fighters swerved and weaved through the sky.

BAMMMMOOOOOSHHHHHHHHHHHH!!!!!!!!!!!!!!!

In an explosion even bigger than the first, a second rocket was blown to smithereens on the screens in front of them.

One of the robot fighters exploded as the anti-aircraft crews caught it in their sights. The two other fighters spun through the air, turned, and came heading back toward the burning launch site.

Three, two, one . . . lift-off.

A sudden bellowing of smoke and flame filled the monitors focused on the two remaining rockets. It was hard to tell whether this was from direct hits from the alien robots or from ignition. And then they saw the two rockets rising, going up up up up.

Please don't let them get shot down now, prayed Myers silently. Please!!

BAMM!!! BAMMM!!!

The two remaining robot fighters both took direct hits from the anti-aircraft batteries and blew to pieces, fragments of metal from them hurtling down onto the launch site.

Meanwhile, the two surviving rockets, with their precious payload of two shuttles and just six Warriors, headed up into the sky and to the edge of the Earth's atmosphere.

Inside their shuttle, Buzz, Mathews, and Garcia had watched the carnage and destruction on their monitors. They exchanged somber looks. Each knew what the other was thinking. Now there are just six of us left. Six to save Earth. It was a tall order.

The shuttle craft disengaged from the last-stage rocket and was suddenly floating free at the upper level of the Earth's atmosphere. For some reason the robot ships had pulled off their attack and let the two remaining rockets continue into space.

"I don't trust this," commented Mathews. "Why aren't they attacking us?"

"Maybe there's some flaw in their mechanism?" suggested Garcia. "Maybe they can't get a fix on us?"

"They're robots," said Buzz. "They can get a fix on

anything. I agree with Chuck, I don't trust this either, but our job isn't about trusting anything. Our job is to find the mother ship and destroy it."

"Shuttle 1 from Shuttle 2!" came the voice of Henry Weiss in their headphones.

"Reading you, Henry," replied Buzz. "How are you boys over there?"

"Still surviving," said Henry. "Which is more than can be said of the other poor sons of guns. Ready to go hunting robots?"

"Go green to that, Shuttle 2," nodded Buzz.

A few minutes later, each of the six Warriors was in his own runabout floating free in space.

Buzz ran through a quick check of the controls. There had been little time to carry out much more than basic tech-run checks on the ground.

Fire guns, he thought, and the guns chitter-chattered, letting off a stream of laser-guided fire. Fire missile 1. Again, the controls responded to his thoughts and the runabout rocked as a missile hurtled into space.

"Easy, Buzz," came Chuck's voice in his headset. "Save some for the enemy."

"Just putting this little old thing through its paces," replied Buzz. "I'd hate to find it doesn't work when I'm face to face with whatever we're up against."

Fly left sixty degrees, he thought, and the runabout turned left at just the right angle.

"Okay," he said. "This baby works. First one to find the mother ship gets a banana."

A flurry through his toughened glass windshield caught his eye, and instinctively Buzz put his craft into a downward dive. He was just in time. A robot fighter had come in at speed and blasted the space where Buzz's runabout had been. Out of the corner of his eye, Buzz saw more robot fighters coming in and two explosions.

"Come in, Warriors!" Buzz called. "Chuck? Danny?"

"Chuck just bought it, Buzz," said Danny's voice. "Watch out, there's . . . !!"

Then Danny's voice vanished, to be replaced by the sound of static.

We're each on our own, thought Buzz.

He thought navigation, moving his small craft forward, then suddenly upward, keeping an eccentric course so that the robot fighters couldn't get a fix on him. The beauty of the brain chip, he thought. Just think and the machine does it. As fast as you can think, that's it.

He soared up into space, and then he saw it. The mother ship.

It was enormous. A large flat disc dominating space, about six kilometers long and a kilometer high. Whoever these aliens are, they must have some serious jamming equipment to keep this thing hidden, thought Buzz.

He was now aware that he was alone. Although he had thrown off his robot fighter pursuers, the other Warriors were still engaged in space combat, wheeling and circling, firing their missiles and guns, and taking flak. More explosions. More Warriors down.

Now Buzz was heading his runabout straight at the huge mother ship. Where to hit it? This thing was so big!

Buzz tuned his mind in to the mother ship's controls, scanning for its machine heart, the center of its operations. Yes, he had it.

Two kilometers ahead was an entry point. In there, Buzz could almost feel the mother ship willing him to enter. It had to be a trap.

As he approached, he saw that the entry point was closing. There was no room to take his runabout in through that closing portal. If he was going to get inside, there was only one way. He had to abandon the runabout. And once he'd done that, there was no way back to Earth for him.

But my mission isn't to get back to Earth, he told himself.

He ran through the last-second checks to his life-support systems to confirm they were working, and then thought "Eject!"

The glass top of the runabout opened and Buzz was thrown out into space. He cartwheeled and spun, and then put himself into a dive for the still-closing portal in the wall of the mother ship. He caught a last glimpse of his runabout as it crashed into the surface of the mother ship, and then he was rolling and tumbling onto a floor. The outer hatch slid shut behind him.

At first there was darkness, then Buzz became aware of a row of dim lights leading further into the giant robot station.

He followed them, wary the whole time, waiting to be attacked. But nothing came at him.

Finally he found himself in a large circular room. It was like being at the hub of an enormous wheel. Banks of screens and read-outs glowed. Lights flickered. There was a constant hum of machines and electricity. He was at the heart of the robot mother ship.

"Welcome, Warrior," said a mechanical-sounding voice. "You are a worthy adversary."

"Better than worthy," snapped Buzz. "I'm here, right where I want to be, and now I'm going to blow this space station to bits."

"I don't think you will," said the voice. "For one thing, you have no explosive devices with you. And this station's automatic defenses are very finely tuned. If you attempt to interfere with any of the equipment, you will die instantly. No, I have another suggestion."

"Which is?" asked Buzz.

"Join us."

"Join you?!"

"You are already half machine. I can sense the microchips in your brain. Your bones and muscles incorporate mechanical hardware."

"Best-quality toughened carbon," admitted Buzz.

"You see," said the voice. "You are one of us already."

"Not the part that matters," said Buzz. "Not my soul."

"The soul does not exist," retorted the voice. "You are just the result of neural connections, as we are. In your case some of them are made up of organic material, but many are inorganic. As I said, you are already halfway to being one of us."

"Thanks for the offer, but I don't think so," said Buzz. "Anyway, I'm on a mission."

"To try and destroy this station," said the voice. "We know."

"So why did you let me get this far?"

"Call it kindred curiosity," said the voice. "We wanted to see what kind of man-machine you were up close. And anyway, you pose no threat. As I said, your microchip remote control cannot affect our systems, our

security systems have seen to that. And if you try to interfere with our control systems physically, you will die. And
you have no weapons, no explosives. You are harmless."

"Not quite," said Buzz quietly. "I'm a weapon."

There was a pause, then the voice said, "I assume this
is your Earthling sense of humor."

Buzz shook his head.

"When they designed us as Warriors, they added in
one very special component. The hardware that your
sensors picked up in my body. My muscles and bones.
Together they make up a bomb. We're supposed to set it
off if we're ever captured with no hope of escape.
Ultimate devastation of the enemy." Buzz looked around
him, at the workings of the robot space station, and
grinned. "This seems a pretty good time to do that,
wouldn't you think? I calculate it would trigger a chain
reaction that would just about finish this station."

"You wouldn't do such a thing," said the voice. "Then
it added: "We wouldn't let you."

"You can't stop me," said Buzz. "All I have to do is
think the password . . ."

He closed his eyes and began to send the message to
the detonator that was his bone and muscle structure. He
had memorized it well these many long years, just in case.

Alpha Delta Gamma Alpha Seven . . .

The explosion ripped through the robot station's control center, gathering momentum as it grew in force . . .

Linda Myers watched the TV monitors. Robot fighter ships were tumbling helplessly out of the sky, crashing into land, smashing into the seas.

"Their control's gone," she said. "They're finished."

"Thanks to your Warriors," muttered General Moffat beside her. He gave a heavy sigh. "And those were the last. Now they're finished."

"No," said Myers softly. "We have the technology. The next generation will be even better." Her voice caught slightly as she thought of Buzz and the others, giving their lives so that Earth could survive. Then she said firmly: "There will always be Warriors."

RATINGS: ROBOTS

CODE OF HONOR: 0

RUTHLESSNESS: 10

WEAPONRY: 10

TACTICS: 7

COURAGE: 0

TOTAL: 27 points

WARRIORS